HER OWN TWO FEET

A Rwandan Girl's Brave Fight to Walk

Meredith Davis
and Rebeka Uwitonze

SCHOLASTIC
FCUS

NEW YORK

Photo credits: 30: courtesy of Natalie Green; 168: courtesy of Marc Simpao; 172: courtesy of Donna Henry; 178: courtesy of Natalie Green; 184: courtesy of Esther Havens. All other photos courtesy of Meredith Davis.

Library of Congress Cataloging-in-Publication Data

Names: Davis, Meredith, (Meredith Lynn) 1971- author. | Uwitonze, Rebeka, author.
Title: Her own two feet : a Rwandan girl's brave fight to walk / Meredith Davis and Rebeka Uwitonze.
Description: New York : Scholastic Focus, 2019. | Audience: Age 8-12.
Identifiers: LCCN 2018041523 (print) | LCCN 2018042859 (ebook) | ISBN 9781338356397 (Ebook) | ISBN 9781338356373 (hardcover : alk. paper)
Subjects: LCSH: Uwitonze, Rebeka. | Clubfoot—Treatment—Juvenile literature. | Children with disabilities—Rwanda—Biography—Juvenile literature.
Classification: LCC RD783 (ebook) | LCC RD783 .D38 2019 (print) | DDC 617.5/850967571—dc23

10 9 8 7 6 5 4 3 2 1   19 20 21 22 23

Printed in the U.S.A.   23

First edition, October 2019

Book design by Becky James

To my family, who said,
"This is my child. We welcome her.
We love her no matter what."
—REBEKA

To Clay, Alayna, Nate, and Benji,
my favorite traveling companions through
this gorgeous world and this wonderful life.
Ndagukunda.
—MEREDITH

TABLE OF CONTENTS

PART THREE: RWANDA

PART ONE

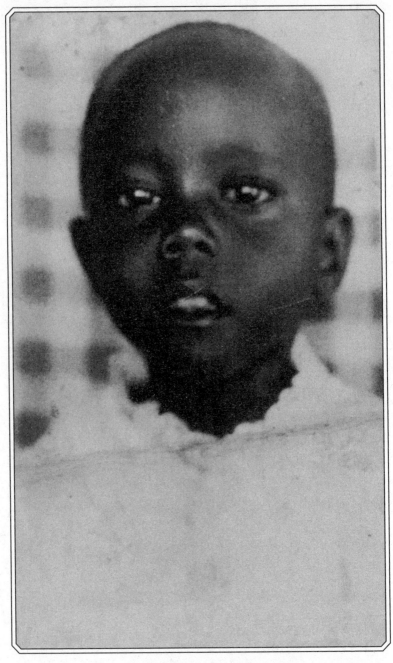

Rebeka, age 3, 2005.

CHAPTER ONE

REBEKA TRACED THE SHAPE OF HER CURLED FEET THROUGH THE blanket that covered her and her little sister, Medeatrece. Everybody was asleep and she needed to go to the bathroom. She wanted to go by herself, without bothering anybody, but she was also afraid. Wild dogs roamed the Rwandan countryside after dark and could easily get into her yard. She heard no howling, so maybe they were nowhere near.

She wriggled out from under the covers and scooted to the end of the bed. It filled up almost the entire room, wedged between two mud walls, with just enough space for the door to swing open.

"Rebeka?"

"Shhhh, Medea. Go back to sleep," Rebeka whispered.

"I awake!"

Rebeka could see the whites of her little sister's eyes in the moon-lit room. She wasn't going back to sleep.

"I have to go to the bathroom," said Rebeka.

"Me, too," said Medea, scrambling from under the covers.

"You're just going because I'm going." Rebeka knew she should tell her little sister to stay put, but it would be nice to have some company. Besides, it was hard to argue with a stubborn two-year-old. Rebeka crawled across the concrete floor of their home, following Medea outside. She lifted one shoulder and then the other, letting her arms swing forward like pendulums and then placing them back down. Her shadow stretched strange in the moonlight.

"I first!" said Medea, skipping to the latrine. Papa had dug a deep hole a good distance from the house so they wouldn't smell the stink and built a small shed around it for privacy.

Rebeka listened carefully for howling or snuffling, but all she heard was the soft breath of a cow and the scratch of a goat moving in his stall. No dogs. She crawled quickly across the red dirt yard. She had long since grown used to the grit that dug into her skin. She'd spent her whole life on the ground. But the tough calluses on her knees and knuckles couldn't protect her if she landed in a pile of goat or cow poo, crawling in the dark. She hoped for the best and kept going.

"Ow!" She brushed the dirt under her knee and picked up something small and hard. Round on one side, pointy on the other, a kernel of maize. Mama had spread a bunch of ears on a blanket to dry in the sun the day before. Rebeka dropped the kernel and crawled the rest of the way to the latrine.

"I done!" said Medea.

"Good job!" Rebeka took a deep breath so she wouldn't smell the stink and crawled inside. It had taken her a while to figure out how to go to the bathroom on her own, but she'd done it. She had figured out how to do lots of things in her first four years of life. After she was done, she and Medea washed their hands in a bucket. The slippery soap was hard to hold, especially since her middle fingers were always curled stubbornly to her palms.

Once the girls were done, they shook their hands dry and hurried back to the house. Their bed was still warm as they settled side by side under the blanket, like two kernels of maize on the cob. Medea reached out and tickled Rebeka's side. She wasn't ready for sleep, not quite yet, and neither was Rebeka. Nighttime was the perfect time to whisper, whether it was secrets or stories or dreams or just silliness.

It all felt important when it was whispered.

> *"I play chickens," said Medea.*
>
> *"Tomorrow," whispered Rebeka. "You can chase the chickens tomorrow. Maybe I will chase, too, someday."*
>
> *"Rebeka crawl chickens."*
>
> *"No, run! Like you, Medea."*
>
> *"How?"*
>
> *Rebeka sighed. "I don't know. Maybe magic. Maybe doctors. Maybe God." She touched her curled toes to Medea's warm feet. "Go back to sleep."*
>
> *"Ndagukunda, Rebeka."*
>
> *"I love you, too, Medea."*

CHAPTER TWO

REBEKA WOKE THE NEXT MORNING TO LIGHT STREAMING through the window. She was alone in the bed. Rebeka scooted to the floor and crawled outside to see where everyone was. Mama stirred porridge in a pot over the fire, and Papa was in the yard, staring out toward the lake. She couldn't see it from the ground, but she knew it was there, the sun shining on the water.

"Why aren't you fishing, Papa?" asked Rebeka.

He picked her up and she shrugged her shoulders to swing her arms up around his neck.

"I had something more important to do today," he said.

More important than fishing? If Papa didn't fish, he had nothing to sell, and without the money he made from his fish, Mama couldn't buy salt or soap or oil.

"Do you remember the stranger who came to visit us?" asked Papa.

"Yes." He had come days ago, sat on the couch, and talked to her

Lake Cyohoha, across from Rebeka's house.

parents for a long time. Mama had carried her away from a game with Medea in the yard to show him Rebeka's feet. He didn't wince when he saw them, even though both curled upside down, and her right foot also twisted backward. She remembered the man's hands were cold but gentle.

"He is a doctor, and he wants you to come to his clinic. He thinks there are therapies that may help your legs and feet. He said he would pay for all your treatments."

Just then, Medea screeched and came running around the house, chasing the chickens like it was just another ordinary day.

"Will it hurt like last time?" asked Rebeka. Someone had come to their house a year ago, saying they could turn her feet, even though the procedure was usually done on babies and she was already three years old. She and Mama went to a hospital where a doctor twisted her feet until the pain made her cry. Then they put casts on to hold them in place, and it hurt so bad she couldn't sleep. When they took off the casts a week later, her feet were still curled.

"That was in the past, Rebeka, and I cannot tell you what the future holds," said Papa. "All I know is what lies before us right now. *Amahirwe aza rimwe.* Chance comes once. We must take advantage of it. You are a whole year older and stronger. Maybe this time it will work. Mama is making your breakfast and then we will go."

Rebeka watched her parents' faces carefully as she ate her porridge. There was something they weren't telling her. Her three older sisters and her brother chatted about what they would do that day, who would watch Medea and who would fetch water and who would mend Papa's ripped shirt. Mama wiped a tear off her cheek, then got up and hurried inside. Rebeka crawled after her, wiggling up the step into their house.

"What's wrong, Mama?"

"It is nothing," she said. "I have happy tears when I imagine these treatments working and my little girl learning to walk. Are you ready?"

Rebeka nodded. "Just let me tell Medea goodbye."

"Why you go?" Medea asked when Rebeka found her. She was sweaty from chasing the chickens.

Rebeka shrugged to swing her arm to Medea's shoulder, then plucked a soft feather off her little sister's cheek.

"So the doctors can fix my feet. Don't worry, I'll be home soon."

"Stay," said Medea. "Play."

"I can't today. Chance comes once." Rebeka held Medea's hand. "Don't chase all the fat off the chickens. We need them to be juicy for Christmas dinner!"

"Christmas!" said Medea. She let go, laughed and clapped, then ran off to play.

Rebeka longed to follow, but it was time to leave. To get to the clinic, they had to travel five miles to the main road, where they could catch a bus, and then walk more miles once they got off again.

"We'll try to flag down a motorcycle to get to the bus," said Mama. She took a piece of cloth and wrapped it around Rebeka's legs and feet to hide them and hold them straight. Then she tied Rebeka to her back. Even though she was four, she was thin and small for her size, and Mama was strong. Papa carried a bag and walked alongside them.

Walls made from dense bushes surrounded most of the houses. Some had clothes or sheets draped over them to dry in the sun. The nicer homes had real walls around them, made from red dirt bricks and covered with thin plaster that peeled and cracked. Everywhere, there were bicycles and people going about their days. After a little while they heard a motorcycle, and Papa flagged it down.

"We need a ride to the main road," he said.

"Untie the girl so she can sit on the seat between you," said the driver.

"It's okay," said Mama. "She can stay on my back."

Rebeka kept her arms tucked in front of her so they were hidden, but the driver was still suspicious. He squinted and said, "The seat is better. Untie her."

And so Mama unwrapped the cloth. When the driver saw Rebeka's twisted legs and feet, he shook his head. "Cursed," he muttered, and drove off.

Papa hugged her. "Ignore him. He doesn't know any better."

Rebeka nodded, though her heart stung. All her life she had tried to ignore people who called her names, but her heart wasn't calloused like her knees and knuckles. It was still tender.

Mama tied her to her back again, and they continued on. They passed women balancing baskets of maize on their heads, with babies strapped to their backs. They passed men pushing bicycles loaded down with sloshing yellow water jugs. And they passed children running and skipping and playing.

Mama's back was hot and wet with sweat by the time they boarded the bus. They walked past full seat after full seat and sat in the back, with Rebeka between Mama and Papa. The heat made her sleepy. She leaned into Mama, closed her eyes, and thought about Medea, who was probably going down for a nap back home.

Usually, she napped at Medea's side. Usually, Medea didn't want to nap, and so they talked until their lids grew heavy and they surrendered to sleep.

> *Medea, my tummy feels funny.*
> *This bus is filled with strangers,*
> *and their strange smells*
> *and their staring eyes that notice my curled feet*
> *dangling from the bus seat.*
> *I close my eyes so I can't see them looking, and pretend I can*
> *   see you stretching across our bed,*

hear you giggling,
feel you tickling me on the side,
and smell the mango juice, dried sticky on your fingers.
I miss you already.
I'll be home soon.

CHAPTER THREE

IT WAS ANOTHER LONG, HOT, DUSTY WALK BEFORE THEY FINALLY got to the clinic.

When they walked through the front door, models of human skeletons hung on either side of the entrance.

"Don't worry, they aren't real bones," Papa said.

But Rebeka still shivered and hid her face in Mama's back. She had seen a dead goat once, picked clean by birds, the bones bleached from the sun. She did not like skeletons. Mama walked up to a nurse sitting behind a desk and said, "My daughter's name is Rebeka Uwitonze. We are here for her treatments."

"Ah, Uwitonze," said the nurse, nodding. "It means 'peaceful.' She must be a good girl."

"She is," said Papa.

"That is good. We have many street children and orphans here to be treated, and some are quite wild. A peaceful child will be appreciated."

Orphans? Rebeka was used to being pitied, and sometimes she even felt sorry for herself. But what if she had no family and had to go through life with her twisted feet all alone?

Mama unwrapped the cloth, and the nurse brought a big wheelchair. It reminded Rebeka of her time in the hospital the year before. Her stomach twisted with fear and worry when they set her on the cracked leather seat.

The nurse pushed her chair down a long hall while Mama and Papa followed. Rebeka peeked through open doors into tiny rooms, each with a small bed and chair in it. The nurse stopped at a room and wheeled Rebeka inside.

"This is where you'll stay while you're here," she said.

"Will I be here overnight?" Papa and Mama hadn't said anything about how long the treatments would take. They were acting strange again, and this time Rebeka was certain there was something they weren't telling her. Mama kissed her cheek. Rebeka used her shoulder to wipe it off. Mama knew she did not like kisses.

"You are my strong, brave girl," she said. She closed her eyes and bowed her head. "God, please help my child. Send a miracle. Turn her feet so she can walk."

Then Papa took her hand and hooked his finger through her tightly curled middle finger. "We love you," he said.

"I love you, too." Why were they being so serious? What were they not telling her?

Mama stood up, smoothed down her dress, and asked the nurse where the bathroom was.

"Follow me," she said. Mama and Papa left, and she was alone. Rebeka looked all around. The room was clean and quiet. Too quiet.

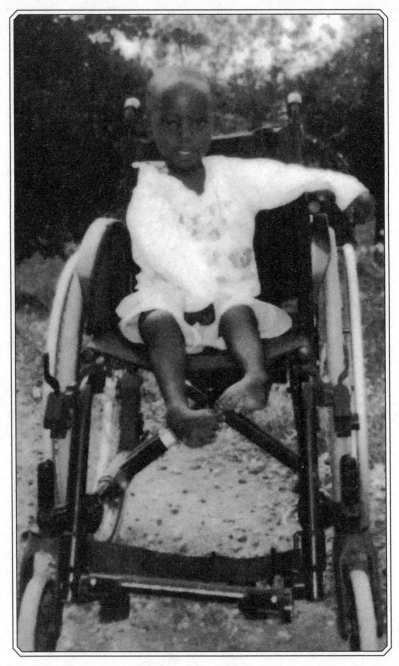

Rebeka, age 4, at the clinic.

"Mama?" she called. "Papa?"

The nurse came back. "Don't worry," she said. "They'll visit soon."

"Visit? Where did they go?"

"They went back to your home," said the nurse in a quiet voice.

She had been left behind? Like an orphan? Angry tears spilled down her cheeks. "Why did they leave me here?"

The nurse bent down and wrapped her in a hug. She was thin and brittle with no soft spots. She was kind, but she was not Mama.

"I'm sorry," she said. "Sometimes a quick goodbye is easier."

But they hadn't even said goodbye. Rebeka choked down a sob. She was four years old and she was alone. "Will they come back?"

"They'll be back next month, on visiting day. It may take a long time to fix your feet, and your parents are needed at home."

Rebeka propped her arm up on her knee to wipe the tears off her cheeks.

"Don't worry, Rebeka. We're going to try to help you," said the nurse.

What if Mama and Papa didn't come back? Maybe she was too much trouble. Maybe it was too shameful, having a daughter with twisted feet. Maybe Mama and Papa were happy to be rid of her.

"Let me know if we can do something to help," the nurse said before leaving.

But the nurse and the doctor could do nothing for her that night when she was alone in her bed, with no Medea by her side. Maybe they could straighten her feet, but they couldn't take away the ache deep down, the hole that only her family could fill.

Medea, are you awake?
There are children up and down this hall, snoring like cows.
The nurses are nice,
there is plenty of food,
but Mama's beans are better.
Tomorrow my treatments start.
I'm afraid they'll hurt, but the worst thing is
when I stretch my leg to find you,
all I find is more bed.

CHAPTER FOUR

EVERY DAY, THE DOCTOR AND NURSES HELPED HER EXERCISE AND stretch to make her legs and ankles stronger. Sometimes they used their hands, and sometimes machines, to try to turn her feet around. The treatments hurt, and it was even worse enduring them alone. After a month, a nurse wheeled Rebeka into the front room, where she saw Mama sitting in a chair.

"Mama!"

The nurse stopped her wheelchair a short distance from her mother, too far to touch her.

"Rebeka!" Mama stood up, but the nurse told her to stay where she was.

"Try to walk to your mama," she told Rebeka.

Walk? Rebeka looked down at her twisted feet. They looked the same as the day she came. She couldn't walk anywhere.

"Come on. Try. Don't you want to hug your mama?"

A tear slipped down her cheek, and across the room, she saw

tears wet Mama's cheeks as well. She would try. She slipped to the edge of the seat, but when her feet touched the floor, they had no strength. She fell out of her wheelchair.

"Rebeka!" cried Mama.

"Mama!" Rebeka crawled across the room, her knees dragging across the cold tile, which was hard against the backs of her hands. Mama reached down, pulled her into her lap, and hugged her tight.

"I'm sorry, Rebeka. I'm sorry."

"Can you take me home, Mama? The treatments aren't working. You can see they haven't changed a thing."

Mama didn't answer, only held her tight. She pressed her cheek against Mama's chest and listened to her heart beat like a drum.

"Where is Papa?"

"Papa will come next month," said Mama. Her chest vibrated with her words. "He needs to take care of things at home, and we only had enough for one bus fare."

Mama stayed for a few hours, but then she had to go.

"Please take me with you," Rebeka begged.

"The doctors say they need more time. Keep being brave and strong," said Mama. "And keep praying. Papa said to remind you, chance comes once. We love you." She had tears in her eyes, but she still left.

Eight long months of treatments passed. Rebeka began to lose hope. Her fifth birthday came and went. It seemed impossible that her feet would ever turn, or that she'd ever walk. Each month it was the same. Sometimes Mama came and sometimes Papa. The nurse always told her to walk and she never could. Her days were filled with painful treatments and her nights with loneliness.

And then one day, her doctor had to leave Rwanda. There was nobody to pay her clinic fees anymore, so Mama and Papa finally took her home.

Papa's arms were strong and familiar as he carried her toward their house. Medea looked so big when she came running out of the house to meet them. She had grown taller and stronger in eight months. She was three years old now, and she had a lot more words.

"Rebeka, I missed you! I love you! Come see the baby goat!"

Rebeka laughed as Papa set her down on the red dirt. Finally, she was home again. She rocked up on her knees and knuckles and followed Medea around the side of the house. She winced as the dirt dug into her skin. Her calluses had softened after spending so much time in wheelchairs at the clinic. The baby goat was adorable, hopping around on tiny, strong legs. Rebeka longed to do the same. Was she not more important than a goat? Still, she couldn't help laughing with Medea as they watched it stumble around. It felt so good to be home.

It didn't take long to get used to her old routines. Day after day, week after week, time passed. Mama had another baby. Rebeka's calluses returned, tough and hard on her knees and knuckles. Her parents didn't have enough money to send their children to school, so her big sisters and brother

Children in line at a water well in Bugesera.

17

worked in the garden and fetched water and helped cook and fish. Even little Medea did chores.

Sometimes, Mama tied her tiny baby onto Medea's back with a scarf wrapped round and round. Rebeka wished she could carry the new baby on her back. As time passed, Rebeka became more and more restless in her broken body. She had her sixth birthday, and then her seventh.

"Mama!" Rebeka called one morning. "Can you carry me to the road?" Maybe something more exciting than chores was happening out there. She could have crawled across their red dirt yard, down the short path and past the garden by herself, but Mama was faster, and she didn't feel like crawling.

"Coming," Mama called. She hoisted Rebeka onto her hip. "You are getting heavy. Someday, I won't be able to carry you anymore."

Too heavy to carry? What would happen to her then? She would be stuck inside or close to the house for the rest of her life.

"Be careful, and stay out of the way of bicycles," Mama said as she set Rebeka down by the road and turned to go back to the house.

"I will."

Mama's words repeated in her head. *Too heavy to carry. Too heavy to carry.* Rebeka picked up a stick and used it to draw a picture of herself in the dirt, an imaginary Rebeka with flat feet who could walk wherever she wanted to go. A group of children raced past, kicking up dust and messing up her picture.

I would be the fastest of all if I could run, she thought as she broke her stick into tiny pieces.

A man came along, his bike clattering down the rough road. On the back he had a bundle of long reeds. It seemed crazy that such a large load could balance on two thin tires. As he passed Rebeka, he stared at her twisted feet and spat in the dirt.

"Hardly human," he muttered as he continued down the road.

Rebeka gritted her teeth and kicked at the wet spot of spit with her bare feet until it was covered in dirt. The bike's tires left a trail, stretching like a long, long snake. She stared at the line, wondering again how such thin tires could support such a large load and such a stupid man. It seemed as impossible as getting up and walking on the tops of her twisted feet.

And yet, the tires held the man.

Could it be that her feet could hold her?

If she could learn how to balance, like a man on a bike, she could get herself off the ground. She wouldn't need to be carried anymore.

"Medea!" she called. "Medea, where are you?"

Medea came skipping around the house. "Here I am!"

"I need your help," said Rebeka. She crawled up the path to the freshly plowed garden where her sister was standing, digging her toes into the soft dirt. "I want to learn how to walk, and you're going to help me."

"But how can you walk?"

Rebeka rubbed her calloused knees. "First, I need to learn how to stand and balance on the tops of my feet. Turn around so I can lean on your back, and grab my hands so you can pull me up."

Medea's hands felt small, but her five-year-old body was strong.

Slowly, slowly, Rebeka stood. All her weight pressed down on the tops of her twisted feet, the tender skin digging into the dirt. She leaned against her sister's thin back, warm from the sun, trying to take some of the pressure off her ankles. When she tried to straighten up, she wobbled and fell.

"Are you okay?"

Rebeka gritted her teeth. "I'm fine. Let's try again."

Medea helped her get up again and again as the sun beat hot in the garden. When they needed a break, Medea got them both mangoes from a nearby tree. The fruit was juicy and sweet and ran down their chins. Rebeka licked her lips, tasting a mixture of mango and salt from her sweat.

"Don't tell Mama or Papa what we're doing," said Rebeka. "I want to wait and show them once I'm stronger and I can walk."

Medea wiped her sticky chin with the back of her hand. "I won't tell, I promise."

Rebeka scraped with her teeth at the bits of mango that clung to the pit until it was smooth and clean. Then she pushed the pit into the soft dirt.

"Let's try again," she said.

She practiced with Medea every day, her strength growing like the tender new shoots of a mango tree. Mama thought they were playing, and had no idea what was really going on. Weeks later, Rebeka was ready for the next step. She rolled over so she was facing the ground. She leaned onto her knuckles and got up onto the tops of her feet, her body bent in half.

"What are you doing?" asked Medea, scrambling to help.

"I want to see if I can get up by myself." Rebeka slowly straightened, her arms swinging as she balanced.

"You're doing it!" said Medea, clapping her hands.

Rebeka bent forward and back, but she stayed upright, like the tall, strong trunk of a mango tree. "One, two, three," she said, counting how long she could stand. She could see the lake from her standing position. "Four, five, six"—her legs shook—"seven, eight . . ." She plopped down on the ground.

She was tired, but she couldn't stop now that she had tasted sweet success. She picked up momentum with each new victory, like a bike rolling down a hill. Medea kept their secret, but sometimes when she looked at Rebeka, she giggled.

"What are you girls up to?" asked Mama.

"Nothing," said Rebeka. "Just playing a game."

A week later, she was able to balance on the tops of her feet for longer than she could count. Each time she made it to twenty, she didn't know what number came next, so she started again at one.

"Let's tell Mama," said Medea.

"Not yet. I want to walk, not just stand."

Learning to walk was much different from getting her balance and standing, but her legs had grown stronger from all the practice, and Rebeka was determined. She dug in, like the roots of a tree, and she would not give up. For months, she practiced. She leaned on Medea like she'd done when she first learned to stand. Medea held on to Rebeka's hands and raised her right leg. Rebeka used her hip to lift her right leg, too. Right, left, right, left; she winced each time

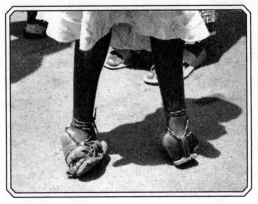

Rebeka's twisted feet in her black sandals.

the tender tops of her feet hit the ground, but she ignored the pain and leaned into Medea. Gradually, she formed calluses on the tops of her feet, like she had on the tops of her hands. After almost nine months of practice, Medea let go and Rebeka took her first steps in the garden on her own.

She felt excitement rise like bubbles in an orange Fanta. She had officially left her life on the ground behind. Everything was going to change now.

"Go get Mama," she said to Medea one afternoon. "It's time."

"Mama!" Medea cried, running out of the garden.

Rebeka was sweaty and dirty and sore, but she pushed herself back up onto the tops of her feet, found her balance, and took some more steps. She had to keep practicing, had to get better so she could walk farther, faster.

"Rebeka!" Mama came around the edge of the bush and ran to Rebeka, scooped her up, and hugged her tight. "Praise God!"

A few days later, Papa came home with a tiny pair of black rubber sandals. They could fit a three-year-old, but since only a small part of Rebeka's feet touched the ground, they were just right. Long, colorful laces threaded through flaps on the sides of the soles.

"Thank you," she said. "I love them."

She practiced wrapping the laces around her ankles and tying perfect bows with her imperfect fingers. Now that she could walk, she felt like there was nothing she couldn't do.

"Do you think you will run someday?" Medea whispered.

Rebeka rolled over in bed, onto her back. "I will do more than run. I will fly."

Medea giggled. "You will grow wings like a chicken!"

"No, no, Medea. A chicken is strong, but it cannot fly." Rebeka stared up into the darkness. "I will grow wings like the hawk, and I will fly up so high I can see the whole world, and the whole world will see me."

"And then you will fly low and leave droppings on Mama's clean laundry!"

Rebeka laughed so loud, Mama came to the door. "Girls," *she said. "It is time for sleep."*

CHAPTER FIVE

Two years after she learned to walk, Rebeka's life didn't look the way she thought it would. She was thankful to be off the ground, but walking on the tops of her feet meant there were still plenty of pointing fingers and *what's wrong with her* whispers. She was still obviously different from everybody else. Her ankles tired easily, and when she walked she swayed from side to side, awkward and clumsy and slow. It was hard enough to still be left behind in races and games, but it got even harder when her parents sent Medea to school. They had enough money for one uniform, one set of shoes, and one tuition. Medea was a good age, she was healthy, and she could walk the long distance to get to the school.

Now I'll never catch up, thought Rebeka when Medea left for her first day of class. *What good is being able to walk if I have nowhere to go?*

She stayed home with Mama and the two babies. Uwiteka was

three now, and Dukudane, her newest little sister, spent her days tied to Mama's back.

"I'll teach you what I'm learning," Medea said when she came home from school that first day. She took out a piece of chalk and showed Rebeka As and Bs and one, two, threes, drawing them on the concrete floor. Rebeka carefully copied them over and over, but she got bored practicing letters and numbers when Medea was gone.

It isn't fair, she thought as she snipped Medea's old homework papers with her mother's scissors one rainy morning. *Not fair, not fair, not fair,* she grumbled to the tap of the raindrops overhead. When she unfolded the paper, it was covered in holes.

"It's a snowflake," said Mama. "I've never seen one, but I've heard they are beautiful. I have an idea." She strung fishing line across the room near the ceiling, and as Rebeka snipped and snipped more papers, Mama hung her creations. The rain stopped and the flakes fluttered in the breeze from the open window.

"They are like people, each one different," said Mama.

But nobody is as different as me, thought Rebeka.

Days passed, and snowflakes accumulated across the tin ceiling that rippled like tiny waves above Rebeka's head. One

Paper snowflakes hanging from the roof of Rebeka's home.

evening, Mama rushed into the house, smudging Rebeka's chalky alphabet and scattering little bits of paper all over the floor.

"I just heard about a new school that will be free, and it's only three miles from here!" she said.

"Free?" Rebeka's heart fluttered like a paper snowflake by an open window. Schools in Rwanda were never free. "So I could go to school, too?"

"Yes! The first two hundred and fifty children to apply will get spots." Mama circled the application date on the paper calendar that was tacked to the wall. When Rebeka told Medea that afternoon, they did a dance, Rebeka swaying back and forth and Medea holding her hands.

When the day finally came, Rebeka's mother strapped Dukudane to her back and took Rebeka and Medea by the hand. "You can walk three miles, can't you, Rebeka? I know it will be hard, but I believe you can do it. If you get to go to this school, there will be days when Papa can't take you on a bike, and you must walk."

"I can do it," said Rebeka. *Chance comes once.* She worked hard to keep up, rolling her hips, picking up one foot and then the other. She had to stop and rest often. As they finally got close, Rebeka heard many voices. Her heart beat fast. She took long strides, stepping as quick as her legs would let her. There was a large group of people already gathered. They made a solid wall of flesh, blocking the path.

"What is she doing here?" somebody yelled.

"That crippled girl doesn't belong! You should leave her at home!"

"Don't take a healthy child's spot by enrolling Rebeka!"

Rebeka felt a tear trickle down her cheek, but she couldn't wipe it away without bending over and propping her arm on her knee. She held her head high instead and stared at the blue sky. Rebeka's mother put her hands on her head and cried. Medea started crying, too.

"What is wrong?" asked a tall man wearing nice clothes, clean and freshly pressed.

"These people don't want my daughter here," said Mama. "But it is not fair to deny her an education because of the way she looks! Her feet may be twisted, but her mind is sharp."

The man bent down and looked Rebeka in the eye. She stared right back. He smiled and picked her up. Rebeka stiffened in his unfamiliar arms. He smelled clean and his arms were strong, but he was still a stranger. The man pushed through the crowd. She watched over his shoulder as her mother and Medea followed in their wake. They got some mean looks, but nobody was bold enough to complain.

"Don't worry," he said once they were inside the building. "I am the headmaster, and I will make sure both of these girls are admitted to Kibenga Primary School and get sponsors to pay for their education."

Sometimes when Papa was fishing, he would catch a fish that was too small to keep. He would work the hook out of its mouth and toss it back into the water. Rebeka felt as if she had just been tossed into freedom, where she could breathe, where she would be allowed to grow. "Thank you!" she told the headmaster. "I will work very hard and you will not be sorry that you have given me this chance!"

Even though Rebeka was nine and Medea was seven, they were

put in the same kindergarten class. They were given new uniforms, red-checkered shirts and red skirts, and strict instructions to keep them clean and wear them only on school days. It was hard to tell the students apart, each one in the same uniform and everyone's head shaved, boys and girls. Rebeka liked that. She got good marks for handwriting and teacher Rehema said she had an excellent memory. She had one hundred and twenty children in her class, ages five to nine years old, but Rebeka felt like she was one of teacher's favorites.

There were times when she could almost forget how different she was. She was learning like everyone else. But then there were the times in the schoolyard when everyone played a chasing game and she had to sit on the side and watch. The times when small huddles of girls whispered and she knew they must be talking about her. She felt as different as the *muzungus* who sometimes visited, clattering down the dirt roads in a big white van to visit sponsored children and see the school. Everything about them seemed different, from the color of their skin, arms covered in hair, to their clothes. Even their smell was unfamiliar.

One day, Medea's sponsor came to visit. The whole family was nervous to welcome a stranger into their home. A visit from a sponsor was a rare treat. Most kids never met the person who paid the fees so they could go to school. This woman had traveled all the way across the ocean to visit.

"*Muzungus!*" cried the neighbor children as the van bumped down the road. There were strangers with white skin waving out the windows of the van.

"*Muzungus! Muzungus!*" Foreigners! Foreigners!

It was nice to have someone drawing stares and attention away from her curled feet. Rebeka stayed close to her father's side as Medea unwrapped the gifts her sponsor, Lizzy, had brought. If she held very still and didn't attract attention to herself, maybe none of the strangers would notice her or her feet. Lizzy had arrived with a bunch of other *muzungus* who had piled out of the van and were hanging out in front of her house. They looked friendly but strange with their blinding white skin.

When a man in an orange shirt smiled at Papa and her, she smiled back and then quickly looked at the ground. Rebeka watched his brown shoes walk across the red dirt toward them. He knelt down and held out a piece of red candy, wrapped in plastic and attached to a short stick. Rebeka rarely had sweets.

"*Murakoze*," she said, but she could not lift her arm to take it. The man didn't understand, and didn't bring the candy any closer.

Papa took it, said, "*Murakoze*," then, "Thank you," in English, and handed the treat to Rebeka.

She bent over to get her mouth to the sweet. It was so good.

She licked it slowly to make it last as she watched Medea jump rope and toss her new ball back and forth with Lizzy. When it was almost gone, she crunched the last bite and chewed on the stick to savor every bit of sweetness.

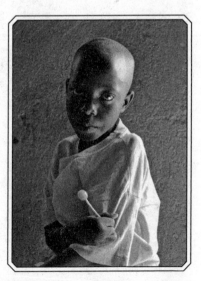

Rebeka, age 9, holding the sucker Clay gave her.

"Rebeka, come walk with us!" Medea called. "Lizzy wants me to show her around."

Rebeka tried to ignore Medea, but her sister wouldn't leave without her. She ran over and took Rebeka's hand. "I want you to come," she said.

"But everyone will stare at my feet," said Rebeka. "I'm tired of stares."

"They stare because it is amazing that you are walking. They stare because they have never seen such a strong girl before."

Rebeka shook her head, but she couldn't help but smile. She held her head high as she walked with Medea to join the others.

As they walked a little ways down the road and Lizzy asked

Left to right in foreground: Lizzy, Mama (with baby Dukudane), Medea, Rebeka, Clay, Papa.

questions and took pictures, she saw Mama talking to the translator and one of the *muzungu* women. Why did Mama look so upset? After Lizzy and the other *muzungus* left, Mama grabbed Papa's arm and led him into the house. Rebeka left the kids who were gathered around Medea, admiring her new jump rope. She leaned against the wall of their home, underneath the open window, and listened. Mama's voice was quiet, but she could still hear her.

"The *muzungu* woman said that when Rebeka grows older and heavier, her ankles and tender skin may no longer be able to support her weight," said Mama. "She may lose the ability to walk."

Rebeka shook her head.

No.

It could not be. She could not go back to crawling.

She hurried away from the house, wishing she had not heard Mama's words, strong like teeth, chomping away at her hopes and dreams, crunching them into little bits like a piece of bitter candy.

> *"Are you sure that's what Mama said?" asked Medea.*
>
> *"I am sure."*
>
> *"Well, maybe the lady was wrong," said Medea. "She was probably wrong."*
>
> *"Yeah, probably."*
>
> *Medea was so quiet, Rebeka thought she had fallen asleep, but then Medea said, "If I could give you my feet, I would."*
>
> *Rebeka found her little sister's hand under the covers and squeezed it. "Medea, I'd never take your feet."*

CHAPTER SIX

W EEKS PASSED. REBEKA FELT AS IF SHE CARRIED A BURDEN
heavier than a water jug inside her, full and sloshing. Fear
and worry spilled into other parts of her life. She tried to eat less so
she wouldn't get too heavy for her ankles, but her stomach groaned
and complained. She was distracted at school, imagining herself as
a grown woman crawling on the ground spotted with cow dung,
people spitting at her and calling her hardly human for the rest of
her life.

Perhaps she could get a wheelchair, or Papa could make her one
from bicycle tires and a chair, but her life did not consist of shiny
flat floors like they had in the clinic. There were dirt roads with
potholes that turned to muck in the rainy season, doorways that
were too thin for a chair to fit through, and a big stone step that led
into the house. Even if a wheelchair worked in her world, she would
still need someone to push her around. She could not lift her arms
and make them spin the wheels.

She must continue walking.

She must.

In the spring, a few months after the *muzungu* visit, a woman came to visit from Africa New Life, the organization that found sponsors for all the students at her school. Rebeka was sitting on the concrete floor, rubbing her sore feet and staring out through the open doorway, when she saw the woman walk across the dirt yard.

"Hello!" said the woman. She peered inside the house. "May I come in and talk to your parents? I have some exciting news to share!"

"Mama," she called. "Someone is here!"

"Come in, come in," said Mama, hurrying to the door. "Let me get my husband."

The woman settled onto the couch across from Mama and Papa. She had a pretty dress and a friendly face. "Do you remember a man who met you when Medea's sponsor came to visit?" she asked, leaning forward and clasping her hands together.

Rebeka nodded. "He was wearing an orange shirt and he gave me a piece of candy."

"His name is Clay, Clay Davis, and when he went home he showed some pictures of Rebeka's feet to her sponsor, Dr. Rice. The Rice family is the one who pays for Rebeka's school tuition."

"I didn't know there was a doctor in Rebeka's sponsor family!" said Mama.

"And Dr. Rice didn't realize his sponsored child had disabilities! He has arranged for doctors in America to examine Rebeka to see if they can help correct her feet."

Mama's mouth fell open, and Papa rubbed his bald head.

"In America?" asked Rebeka.

"If the doctors decide they can help you, they will treat you for free," the woman said, turning to Rebeka and smiling. "And you can stay with the Davis family while you are in America."

"Doctors have told us before that they could help Rebeka, but they couldn't," Mama said, shaking her head.

"Nobody is making any promises," said the woman. "Except to examine her. They will only treat Rebeka and do surgery if they think it will work. They have to see her before they can decide."

"Surgery?" asked Papa.

"Maybe," said the woman. "They'll have to wait and see. She could be in America just a few weeks, or she may be there for a year. It all depends on what the doctors say."

A year?

"America," said Mama, as if it was just now sinking in. "They want to fly Rebeka to America?"

"Chance comes once," said Papa as he took Mama's hands.

Rebeka stood up and walked across the room, out the door, and into the yard, where Medea was drawing pictures with a stick. She remembered the day her parents left her at the clinic for eight long months. Now they wanted to send her away again.

"Rebeka, why are you crying?" Medea asked.

She told her sister everything the woman had said.

"All the way to America?" asked Medea. "That's so far. I don't want you to leave again."

"I don't want to leave you, either." She sat down and wiped her wet cheeks on her knee. She leaned into Medea so their shoulders and legs touched.

"Look, there's a plane," said Medea, pointing to the sky. Rebeka tilted her head back to see. "If you went to America, you'd fly in one of those."

It looked like a tiny silver toy in the sky. The white puffy trail it left behind wasn't so different from the trail a bike left behind in the dirt.

"I used to think it was crazy that two bicycle tires could hold a man and his heavy load," Rebeka said. "Almost as impossible as walking on the tops of my feet."

"But you did it!" said Medea.

"I did. With your help, I did it."

Was it crazy to think a small silver toy of a plane could fly her across the ocean, where doctors could make her curled feet straight? If they could, it would change her whole life. What was one year, compared with a whole lifetime of walking?

"If the doctors can help me, the way you helped me, how can I refuse?" she asked. "I must take this chance, even though it is hard. Even though I will have to leave home again."

She stood up and Medea wrapped her arms around Rebeka's waist. "You are right," she said. "I don't want you to leave, but you are right."

Together they walked back into the house and found Mama and Papa and the woman still talking.

"When do I leave?" Rebeka asked, before she could start crying again.

There were days and weeks and months of waiting and working. There were trips to the city and forms to sign and permissions to get from people in government. She met her translator, Anna, who would travel with her and stay in America for a few days so Rebeka could ask questions and understand what was happening. She received an album filled with photos of the people she would live with in America. She recognized the man who had given her the candy. *Clay, Clay,* she said over and over, so she wouldn't forget his name.

"If you go to America, you'll never return," she overheard one of her neighbors warn. Never return? Why? Rebeka felt panic begin to rise, making it hard to breathe.

"Don't worry. They are just jealous that you get to go to America," Papa said when she told him.

Rebeka looked down at her feet as the panic drained away. "Nobody has ever been jealous of me before."

Someone from Africa New Life bought her a suitcase and filled it with more clothes than she'd ever owned before. Mama made matching dresses for her and Medea that they wore for a special family picture.

The day before it was time to go, Rebeka folded her dress carefully and put it in her suitcase, and Mama added a small blue handkerchief, stitched with Kinyarwanda words.

Uzandindishavu Nzakubebishema

Rebeka ran her finger over the letters, stitched with orange thread. *Protect me from grief. I will be your pride.* She hoped she would not be too sad, and she hoped to make her parents proud.

Papa put the suitcase by the front door, and her family gathered for one last meal together. Papa had killed a chicken for the special

Left to right, back row: Esperanze, Magwaneza, Papa, Mama, Uwase, Emmanuel; front row: Medeatrece, Uwiteka, Rebeka, Dukudane.

occasion, and there was orange Fanta. It was a treat usually reserved for Christmas Day. There were also beans and rice and mango, perfectly ripe, from a nearby tree.

"What if it hurts?" asked Rebeka.

Mama put down her bowl and pulled Rebeka into her lap. "I knew before you were even born that something was different from my other pregnancies. At first, you moved inside me like all the others had, kicking and squirming, but at eight months, you began to roll. The night you were born, you did not cry, though your body was curled like a snail. It looked as if your hands and feet were bound with twine, and the cord that connected us was already

37

severed. I was shocked. We did not understand, but of course we still loved you. You were our child. We gave you the name Uwitonze, Rebeka Uwitonze, because you were a peaceful child, despite all the hardship you faced."

Her older sisters and brother nodded their heads.

"I remember."

"Me, too. You hardly ever cried, Rebeka."

"You carry that peace with you still, in here," Mama said, touching Rebeka's chest. "So do not be afraid."

"Yes, Mama." She had heard the story before, many times. She didn't like the next part.

"In those early days," Mama continued, "it was very hard. The neighbors told me that I should wrap you in a blanket so tight you couldn't breathe. They told me to leave you by the side of the road and let you die."

Papa shook his head and clucked his tongue. Rebeka waited for the next part, her favorite part.

"I couldn't do it. I looked into your eyes and I knew that you deserved a chance at life."

Rebeka leaned closer to Mama, thankful to be alive no matter what her feet looked like. Mama hugged her tight and rocked her like she was a baby.

"You lived for a reason. You taught yourself to walk, and now you will do this new hard thing, leaving your family to go to America at nine years old. It may be scary and painful at times, but it will be wonderful, too. Store up all your new stories inside yourself, Rebeka. Bring them home to us."

"I can't believe you leave tomorrow," said Medea.

"Neither can I."

They faced each other in bed, their heads on their pillows,
* the moonlight shining through the window.*

"Are you excited?"

"Yes."

"Are you afraid?"

"Yes." A tear ran over the bridge of Rebeka's nose and
* dropped onto the sheet.*

"I'm going to miss you so much."

"I'm going to miss you more."

They were quiet after that. Rebeka listened to Medea's
* breath slow down. When she turned over in her sleep,*
* Rebeka snuggled close to her little sister, memorizing her*
* shape and her smell, and the sound of the Rwandan night*
* outside.*

PART TWO

CHAPTER SEVEN

THE NEXT EVENING, AT THE AIRPORT, SHE CLUNG TO MAMA AND Papa, crying. The translator, Anna, was waiting with her son, Danny, who was in a stroller.

"We must go," said Anna. "I'm sorry, but we have to leave now or we'll be late for our flight."

Papa let go first, then Mama.

"We love you," they called.

Rebeka tried to stop crying so she could say goodbye, but she was so full of sadness no words spilled out, just tears. As she went through the security line and lost sight of her parents, she felt as if her heart were splintering like a piece of chalk dropped on the concrete floor. She tried to ignore all the stares of strangers while she walked beside Anna on the tops of her feet. She looked through the big windows of the terminal and saw the silver airplane that would lift her high above the earth and carry her across the ocean.

Fear replaced sadness. Silence replaced tears.

When it was time to board, she followed Anna outside. A set of stairs had been rolled into place in front of the door to the airplane. A stranger, someone dressed in an airport uniform, carried her up the stairs and put her down in the airplane. Anna walked along the aisle and stopped at a middle row.

"This is our spot," she said.

Rebeka sat in a big, smooth seat and carefully watched how to buckle her seat belt. The tiny oval windows were too far away to see much when they took off, but that was okay with Rebeka. She closed her eyes tight and prayed they wouldn't crash as the plane picked up speed. Her stomach dropped when they rose into the air. Her ears hurt. Danny started to cry.

"Rebeka," said Anna, shaking her arm. Rebeka opened her eyes. "Try to yawn. It will help your ears."

Rebeka opened her mouth wide, waiting for the yawn, which made Danny laugh. The yawn came, filling her chest and popping her ears, and then she felt a little better. She studied all the people sitting around them and wondered where they were going. When the food came, Anna helped her put her tray down since she couldn't lift her arms. She looked at the food but couldn't eat, because she didn't have room to bend all the way to her tray and she couldn't lift her food to her mouth. She looked at Anna, who was busy trying to keep Danny from throwing Anna's food and drink all over the plane.

"I'm sorry, Rebeka," Anna said. Then she leaned over in her seat and asked the stranger on Rebeka's left something in English. The woman nodded and smiled at Rebeka, then picked up a fork, put a small bite of potato on it, and held it to Rebeka's lips. She took a bite but shook her head when the woman held up another. She didn't like being fed like a baby, and she wasn't very hungry anyway.

Eventually, she slept.

By the time she woke up, she wasn't afraid of flying anymore. If they hadn't crashed yet, it was probably okay. And the airplane was so fancy. There were tiny TV screens on the backs of the seats that showed movies. Anna helped her put small pieces of plastic in her ears and then she could hear the voices and the music. She didn't understand what they were saying since it was in English, but it was still wonderful. And there was a toilet on the plane, and a sink that turned on and off with the press of a button. A woman brought her soda with a straw so she didn't have to lift her cup to take a sip. When Anna said she'd had enough, there was still clean water whenever she asked for it, in a fresh new cup each time. How Mama would have loved that fresh water, simple as asking, instead of walking miles to the well to fill her yellow jug.

They changed planes and flew again, then changed to yet another plane and flew even farther. She woke and slept and woke and slept until the only way to tell if it was day or night was to look out the window to see if the sun was up. As she buckled her seat belt for the last flight of their thirty-hour journey, she tried to swallow the lump of fear that had lodged in her throat again, big as the pit of a mango. What would happen to her when she got to America? Would the Davis family leave her alone in the hospital like her parents did in the clinic? Would the doctors be able to help her? Would it hurt?

She was so far from her family and her friends, her house and her lake that shone in the afternoon sun. She was far from her concrete floor, dusted with chalk letters, and her snowflakes that hung from the ceiling, each one different. She wished she could close her eyes and sleep again, but sleep was as far away as her home and her school and her family and everything she loved.

Rebeka's house in Bugesera.

"You're so quiet," said Anna as she helped Rebeka pull the seat belt tight. A long, loose canvas tail hung off the edge of her seat. "Are you nervous? Excited?"

Rebeka shook her head but didn't speak. She didn't know how to put her feelings into words. She was both of these things. More than anything, she felt alone, even with Anna and Danny by her side, and she felt sick. Sick for her home.

Is it night in Rwanda, Medea?
It's night here,
up in the sky.
There is a man sleeping across the aisle with his mouth
 wide open.
Baby Danny is sleeping on Anna's lap,
 and Anna is asleep, too.
Am I the only one awake in the whole wide world?

CHAPTER EIGHT

WHEN THE WHEELS OF THE PLANE TOUCHED DOWN WITH A squeal and a jerk in Austin, Texas, it was three in the morning and dark outside. Anna rubbed her eyes and yawned and gathered all their things. Danny was wide awake and laughing. They waited until everyone else was off, and then Rebeka walked down the aisle on the tops of her feet, rocking side to side. Her arms brushed the smooth seats, so blue and perfect. The fizzy soda she sipped earlier bubbled in her belly. Her gut twisted with worry, and her brain felt foggy from so many hours in the air, between worlds.

They didn't have to walk down any stairs when they left the plane. Instead, they walked down a long tunnel. At the end, an airport employee was waiting for them with a wheelchair.

"I know you can walk, but I think a wheelchair will be faster," said Anna. "We need to find the Davises and get to bed."

A wheelchair was fine with Rebeka. She was tired. The woman rolled Rebeka through the quiet airport, following behind Anna, who was pushing Danny's stroller. All the shops were closed, and there were almost no people except the ones who got off their plane. Everything looked clean and shiny and new, not a bit of trash on the ground.

She rubbed the lines on her black corduroy pants. They were soft from years of wear, passed down and down until they ended up in the secondhand store in her village. They did a good job of hiding her legs. She tucked her hands in and out of the long sleeves of her jacket, trying to decide which looked more strange, no hands or *her* hands, calloused on the backs with her middle fingers resting on her palms.

It didn't matter, really. She was in a wheelchair, she couldn't speak English, her head was shaved, and her curled feet were fully visible in her sandals, poking out from the bottoms of her pants. She was going to seem strange to these Americans no matter what.

They stopped at the elevator. "We'll meet you at the bottom," said Anna. "I'll take Danny on the escalator."

The woman pushing the wheelchair said something in English that Rebeka couldn't understand. When the elevator doors opened they went inside and the woman pushed the button with a number one on it. As they went down, Rebeka felt her stomach drop the way it had in the airplane. At the bottom, the elevator dinged and the doors opened, but she didn't see the same thing she'd seen when they went in. There was a group of people standing there, smiling and waving. They all had white skin. Where was Anna?

Rebeka ducked her head and stared at the shiny white floor, flecked with bits of black and gray, as she was wheeled into the middle of the huddle of strangers.

"Rebeka, we're so excited you're here!"

Rebeka, wereso exci toodyer ear!

"Welcome to Texas!"

Welk umto Texas!

"It's August, why are you wearing that jacket? You're going to be hot outside!"

Itsah gust, wire yewwareing at jack it? Yergoing tubeee hotowside.

Almost all the English words were nonsense to Rebeka. She'd only learned a few in Rwanda, and she wasn't used to hearing them spoken so fast. She stared at the floor. Some of the strangers leaned down and gave her hugs. Hair tickled her cheek and smells filled her nose with scents she couldn't identify.

"Rebeka," said a woman. She bent down to look in her eyes. "*Amakuru?*"

Rebeka glanced up when she heard the familiar word, and saw a familiar white face. Natalie worked with Africa New Life. She had been to Rebeka's home, and she knew a little Kinyarwanda.

"*Ni meza,*" she said in answer to Natalie's question, even though she wasn't fine. She was terrified, but she had to be brave. She had promised Papa. "Hello," she said, looking all around the circle of people surrounding her. "Hello" was the first English word she'd learned in school.

"Hello!" said a girl with her hair pulled back like a tail, and a boy with short blond hair that bristled, and a lady with a camera swinging around her neck. Everyone was smiling at her. She kind of recognized some of them from the pictures they'd sent, but in the pictures they stayed still so she could study them and practice their names. Here they were passing Danny around and helping Anna with the bags, a swirl of activity with her at the center.

49

Another woman knelt down on the floor so she was face-to-face with Rebeka. "Meredith," she said, putting her hand on her chest. Rebeka nodded. She understood that the woman's name was Meredith and she remembered her from the pictures. She was the mother in her host family.

"That's Clay," said the woman, pointing to a man in a blue shirt. He was the man who'd given her the candy. "And that's Alayna." The girl in a white T-shirt and black shorts, her hair pulled back like a tail, smiled a wide smile. Rebeka remembered her from the picture, the only daughter of the Davis family, and the oldest child. She felt a pang of sorrow as she thought of Medea back home.

"There's Benji," Meredith said, and the boy with short blond hair, wearing an American flag T-shirt, smiled and waved. He was the youngest boy in the host family, about her age. Maybe he would like to draw with chalk on the concrete floor.

"And that's Nate," said Meredith. Nate's hair was a little longer than Benji's, and he was taller.

"Hi!" said Nate.

"Hello," Rebeka said again.

"Hi, I'm Ani," said a tall girl with long blonde hair. This was one of the girls in her sponsor family, the ones who paid her tuition. Her father was Dr. Rice, the one who brought her here. Rebeka knew from their letter that she and Ani had the same birthday.

"Hello," said Rebeka. Then all of a sudden, more English words came to her, words she recited each day in teacher Rehema's kindergarten classroom. "My name is Rebeka," she said proudly.

Everyone laughed, and she ducked her head. She was so stupid!

Of course they knew who she was. Why else would they be here in the dark morning hours?

"We need a picture!" said Ani's mother, who had blonde hair just like Ani. She held up her camera, and everyone gathered around Rebeka.

"*Seka!*" said Natalie. "*Seka cyane!*"

Rebeka tried to smile big like Natalie said, but her lips would not curl up. The Davises, Ani, Natalie, Anna, and baby Danny circled around her, leaning down so they were at her level.

After the picture they all went outside, into the dark morning. Ani and her mother said goodbye.

Left to right, back row: Alayna, Ani, Meredith, Benji, Anna, Nate; front row: Rebeka, Natalie, Danny.

"We'll see you later. Get some rest!"

Rebeka nodded even though she didn't understand what they'd said. Would she ride on a motorcycle to get to the Davis house? How many would it take to carry them all?

Clay pushed her wheelchair to a big car, lifted Rebeka onto the seat, and helped her buckle her seat belt.

A car!

Rebeka looked all around: two seats in front, a bench that seated three in the middle, and space in the back for suitcases. Anna and Danny sat on the same row as her, and Alayna was up front. Clay and the boys got into a different car.

Two cars! Where was the driver?

Meredith got into the seat with the steering wheel and started their car.

Meredith could drive? As she stared out the window, Rebeka tried to pretend it was normal for a mother to drive a car. There were no motorcycles or bicycles to dodge, and no people walking on the road. It was wide enough for six lanes of cars, and it was smooth, not bumpy. She looked up but the stars were lost in the bright streetlights. They flashed past so fast they blurred into one long line. Meredith and Alayna asked her questions and Anna translated.

"How was your trip?" asked Alayna.

Rebeka had no words for the last thirty hours. "*Sawa*" was all she said. Good. Fine.

"How are you feeling?"

How did she feel, so many miles from her family and home? She was afraid if she said too much, she'd start to cry. "*Sawa*," she said again.

Anna laughed a tired laugh. "I think Rebeka is sleepy. Maybe she'll be more talkative tomorrow."

But Rebeka didn't feel sleepy. She watched out the window intently, trying to see where they were going. They weren't in the city anymore. There were trees and hills on either side of the car. The car turned onto a curvy road that crept up, up, up, and then down, and finally they made one last turn onto a paved path that ended at a big, two-story building. Beyond a courtyard wall Rebeka saw lights flickering next to a large wooden door, and up high, there were tiny windows, curved at the tops. Meredith pulled the car into a big room with a concrete floor. As the big door rolled up, white lights turned on.

"We're here!" said Meredith. "We're home!"

"She says we are home," explained Anna. "This is their house."

Rebeka waited for someone to help her out of the car. For just a moment, she was alone as everyone opened and shut their doors to get out, long enough to think about home, and Medea, and all she had left behind.

> *Medea,*
> *Meredith says we are home,*
> *but "we" is not me.*
> *My home will always be red dirt roads,*
> *mangoes in the trees,*
> *beans and rice for dinner,*
> *and you by my side when it's time for bed.*

CHAPTER NINE

MEREDITH LIFTED HER OUT OF THE CAR AND SHE FOLLOWED Benji through the big room with the concrete floor, wondering where the beds were. Benji opened a door that led to a long hall paved with red stones. There were round electric lights pushed up into the ceiling so that she could see the light but not the bulbs unless she got right under them and looked up.

"Your room is upstairs," Benji said.

She didn't understand any of his words, but she followed him when he turned and walked all the way down the hall to the bottom of a staircase. The stairs were made of wood polished to a shine, and there was a black metal railing to hang on to. Only she couldn't hang on, because she couldn't raise her arm, and even if she could, there was no way she could climb up all those stairs. The family followed them inside, their voices loud and excited in the hall.

"I'll carry you," said Clay, and he lifted her onto his hip. She held herself stiff and silent as they went up the stairs. "You're going to sleep with Alayna in her room."

Anna translated what Clay had said. Rebeka was glad she wouldn't sleep by herself. The last time she'd done that was at the clinic when she was four. The whole family followed them up. At the top of the stairs, Clay put her down and she followed Alayna into a room with bright turquoise walls. There was a bed set into the wall like a giant couch, with bookshelves on both sides. Alayna pulled a big drawer out from underneath the bed, and it had a whole other bed inside. Rebeka sat on it and bounced up and down. So soft and springy!

"Time for a bath," said Anna.

"A bath?"

"You've been traveling for almost two days. You need to wash yourself before you get into that nice, clean bed. Follow me."

At home they fetched water from the lake for baths, and she stood in the yard while Mama poured it out of the yellow jug onto her head. When the water hit the red dirt, it splashed muddy water on her legs, so she washed those last. The water wasn't warm, and getting wet outside always made her shake and shiver.

Here, there was a separate room with a big tub and a sink and a toilet. There were tiny black-and-white tiles on the floor and a soft white rug. Anna shut the door and began to fill the tub with water. She helped Rebeka undress and lifted her in so she wouldn't slip and fall. The white tub was smooth and clean, and the water was wonderful and warm. Anna rubbed a soft rag on her back, but when she tried to wash her head, Rebeka said, "I can do it." She bent over, nose to knees, and scrubbed her head, scratching hard with her fingernails. When she was done, Anna helped her dry off with a big, fluffy towel.

"We bought Rebeka some pajamas," Meredith said through the closed door. "Does she want to wear them?"

"Thank you," said Anna. She opened the door a crack, and Meredith handed her a nightgown.

"Is that for me?" asked Rebeka.

"It is. It is a gift from the Davises. Be sure to tell them thank you."

"*Murakoze!*" Rebeka said through the door. This was nothing like she had expected. She had pictured doctors and a hospital and maybe casts, but she hadn't given much thought to the in-between times, when she was just living in America. "They wear pretty dresses to bed?" she asked Anna. "Why don't I save it for tomorrow?"

"You will have different clothes for the day." Anna pulled the paper tag off the nightgown and helped Rebeka put it on. It was thin and soft, with a bright flower print. Rebeka rubbed the material between her fingers, her first brand-new clothes from a store.

"I'm going to put Danny to bed," said Anna. "Meredith can help get you in bed. Good night, Rebeka. You are a brave little girl." She kissed Rebeka's cheek.

Rebeka shrugged her shoulder and wiped her cheek with it.

"You don't like kisses?" asked Anna.

"Not really."

"Then a hug," she said, and she held Rebeka close for just a moment. Then she yawned. "I'll see you in the morning."

"Let's brush your teeth," said Meredith as she came into the bathroom.

Without Anna she had no idea what Meredith was saying, but she was holding a toothbrush, so Rebeka could guess. Before she could swing her arm to grab it, Meredith knelt down and held the toothbrush to Rebeka's lips. She didn't like it, but she opened her mouth. Meredith gently brushed her teeth. When she was done, Rebeka leaned over the sink and spat hard. She was not a baby. She could brush her own teeth. Meredith filled a cup with water from the tap and held it to Rebeka's lips. Rebeka sipped and spat again. She was too tired to try to make Meredith understand.

"Time for bed! I bet you're exhausted," said Meredith.

Rebeka followed her out of the bathroom and plopped down on her bed in the big drawer. Alayna was in the other bed, smiling and yawning. Rebeka's eyes were heavy, but before she could lay her head on her pillow, a small white dog ran into the room.

Her heart raced and she screamed as she remembered the wild dogs she'd heard and seen in Rwanda. Their shadows were swift and their jaws were fierce. Her family had lost chickens to the dogs, and one time a goat. She tried to scramble away as the dog jumped on the bed. She couldn't use her arms to protect her face, so she buried it in the blanket.

"Molly, get down!" yelled Alayna. She picked up the dog. "I'll take Molly downstairs."

Their words, the dog, it was all confusion to Rebeka. She waited as she heard a whimper and then bare feet thudding down the wood floor in the hall. Then she lifted her head.

"I'm sorry Molly scared you," said Meredith. Her green eyes looked worried. "She won't hurt you. She was just excited."

Shewo nt hurtew. Shewas justex ited.

Rebeka's heart was still beating fast. Meredith yawned. "Let's go to bed."

Letsgo tube ed.

She turned out the light and held up the covers so Rebeka could get underneath. Rebeka closed her eyes. The sheets were cool. The bed felt empty with only her body in it. She missed Medea.

Stitching on Rebeka's handkerchief; translation: "Protect me from grief. I will be your pride."

"Good night," said Meredith.

Goo dn ite. Rebeka closed her eyes and pretended to be asleep when Alayna came back. Beside her bed, on the floor, was her suitcase. She still hadn't opened it, but she knew that folded neatly inside was the small blue handkerchief Mama had made, stitched with words of protection against grief. She swallowed hard and squeezed her eyes to hold back her tears. She would make Mama and Papa proud. She would be brave. She wondered if the handkerchief would smell like Mama, and home. If she got it out, it would only make it harder to hold her tears inside. Better to stay quiet and still, and wait for the morning sun.

> *Medea,*
> *There is a wild dog in this house.*
> *Nobody said anything about a dog.*
> *They gave me a new dress to sleep in,*
> *and I sat in a big white tub to take my bath.*

Water gushed right out when Anna turned the knob,
and it was warm,
and my bed is cozy,
but Alayna snores.
No matter how nice this house is,
with its electric lights and its stairs and its beds in drawers,
it will never be as nice as our house,
because you're there.

CHAPTER TEN

A FEW HOURS LATER, REBEKA OPENED HER EYES TO SUNSHINE streaming through wooden blinds, falling in stripes across her bed.

"Good morning," said Alayna. She was lying in the bed above Rebeka, her head propped up on her hand.

Rebeka blinked, trying to remember where she was and who that girl was, and it all came back to her in a whirl of airplane and car ride and warm bath and dog jumping on her bed. She turned over and put her feet on the ground, then pushed up with the back of her hands to stand. Alayna jumped out of bed, but Rebeka closed the bathroom door firmly behind her before Alayna could follow her in. She would take care of herself.

First she used the toilet. It was wonderful to sit down instead of trying to balance over a hole. When she was done, she opened the door. Alayna was waiting right outside. Rebeka picked up her toothbrush and held it firmly. Bracing her arm on the counter, she brought her mouth down and brushed her teeth by moving her head back and forth, scrubbing hard, hard, hard, just like she did at home. Then she turned on the water and picked up the cup, but she couldn't reach the stream of water and keep her elbows on the counter for support. They kept slipping into the sink.

"Here, let me help," said Alayna. Rebeka couldn't understand the words, but she let Alayna take the cup and fill it with water.

"*Murakoze*," said Rebeka. Alayna held the cup to Rebeka's lips, but Rebeka shook her head.

"Not thirsty?" asked Alayna. She set the cup down.

Rebeka slung her arm up to the counter, pulled the cup to the edge, and tipped it with her lips to take a sip. Then she used her mouth to set it upright again. Even though her feet were curled and her arms were limp, she could do some things for herself. She was no baby.

"Good job!" said Alayna. She smiled at Rebeka in the mirror. "Let's get dressed." She held up a red sundress with big flowers on it.

Another new dress?

"*Murakoze!*" Rebeka said. She bent double so her nightdress fell over her head and to the ground. When she straightened back up, Alayna put the red dress over her head and pulled her arms under the straps.

"You look great!" Alayna pointed to the mirror on the wall.

Rebeka stared at her shaved head, her thin shoulders, her limp arms, and her twisted feet, then turned and walked out of Alayna's room and down the hall. She didn't like the mirror. She waited at the top of the stairs for Alayna, who picked her up and carried her down.

She could see the house better now that it was day. Wood floors stretched down hallways and across large rooms filled with soft couches and a big table with ten chairs. The kitchen gleamed white and silver and clean.

"Good morning!" said Meredith and Clay. They were sitting on stools, eating.

"Hello!" said Rebeka, practicing her English word. Alayna set her down and picked up a framed picture. Rebeka's heart leapt like a baby goat when she saw that it was her family, the picture where she and Medea wore their matching dresses.

Alayna pointed at Rebeka in the picture and said, "Rebeka," then pointed at Medea and asked again, "What's her name?"

Rebeka swung her arm up to the picture and pointed to Medea. "Medeatrece," she said. It was Medea's full name, the one Mama used when she was introducing Medea to strangers. Alayna said it all wrong. Rebeka giggled, then repeated her name, "Medeatrece." She waited until Alayna got it right before she pointed to each of her other sisters and her older brother, saying each of their names slowly and carefully. It felt good, being the one who knew how to say the words right.

Suddenly, two dogs scampered into the kitchen, both white and hairy with nails that clicked on the wooden floor. Rebeka hid behind Alayna, clutching her shirt. Alayna reached around and picked her up as Clay and Benji hurried over to get the dogs. Clay held his dog belly up, rubbing her pink spotted skin. She looked like a little hairy baby. These were not like the wild dogs of Rwanda.

"This is Molly," said Clay, looking at the dog in his arms. "That's Maggie," he said, nudging his chin at the dog Benji was holding.

Rebeka shimmied out of Alayna's arms and swung a hand up to scratch behind Molly's ears. Molly licked her hand with a warm, smooth, pink tongue.

"Molly!" Rebeka shrieked, and then laughed.

Meredith went to the kitchen and turned a dial. A flame came up out of a hole, and she set a pan on top of it. There were five other holes, enough room for six cooking pots in all! A package of eggs was sitting on the counter, and a bowl with mangoes and bananas and other fruits she had never seen before. Rebeka's stomach rumbled.

"Do you want a piece of fruit?" asked Clay, pushing the bowl toward her.

Rebeka reached for a small yellow fruit.

"A lemon? You don't want a lemon. It's sour."

Clay made a funny face and Rebeka laughed, but she still grabbed the lemon. She had never tried this fruit, but she loved the color, bright as the petals of sunflowers in Rwanda.

"Okay," said Clay. "If you say so."

He got a knife, cut the fruit in half, and handed her a piece. She dug her front teeth into the juicy flesh and her eyes immediately watered. She dug her teeth in deeper, scraping the inside of the thick skin and raking the sour fruit into her mouth. She would be brave and strong and eat this strange fruit. After all, *chance comes once.* She wanted to experience as much as she could in case the doctors said they couldn't help and she was sent home soon. But the fruit made her eyes water and her lips pucker. Once was enough. She would never do it again. She tried to take a bite of the thick skin but decided it was like the outside of an avocado, too tough to eat.

"Wow," said Clay, when she handed him the empty yellow fruit. "I'm impressed."

"He said he's proud of you," said Anna as she came in with Danny. Rebeka smiled at Clay and bent down to rub Danny's head. He looked up at her and then started crawling as they all sat down for breakfast. Clay brought her a plate filled with eggs and mango cut into slices. She ate everything, and when Clay gave her more eggs, she ate them, too. Her stomach felt round and full in a way it seldom felt at home. She leaned back in her chair and looked around the room.

"Danny!" she yelled. He was stuck in a hole in the wall.

"Oh no, he's trying to go through the dog door!" said Meredith. Anna laughed and got up from the table to get him. Rebeka got up, too, so she could investigate this hole.

"It's a little door just for the dogs," explained Anna.

Next to it was a big door that led into the backyard. She swung her arms and shrugged her shoulder just right so that her hand landed on the doorknob. Then she leaned forward, pushed the handle down, and stepped outside. Alayna followed her.

"Rebeka, hold on, let's put on your shoes!" called Meredith.

She sat down on the tile porch and Meredith knelt beside her. She reached out and touched one of Rebeka's curled feet, looking closely at the callus on top, rough as an elephant's hide. Rebeka watched Meredith's face closely to see if there was disgust, but all she saw was curiosity. Rebeka showed Meredith how to wrap her laces just right around her ankles and tie them tight. Then she stood up and Alayna took her hand. They walked across the grass, past what looked like a giant fishing net stretched tight on a metal frame, to a sandy beach by the water's edge.

It was beautiful and quiet in the shade of giant trees, until she heard a deep roar. A boat sped around the bend, slicing through the water and sending a spray of droplets in a big arc. Rebeka lurched across the grass as she hurried back toward the house, her heart beating fast.

"Rebeka, it's okay," said Alayna, but Rebeka didn't stop until she was inside.

America was filled with strange and unfamiliar things, dogs and lemons and boats. All she wanted at that moment was her own

Rebeka on the beach behind the Davis house.

home, and her own family. She walked to the picture of her family, tipped it forward, and kissed her mother's face. The glass felt cool on her lips, nothing like her mother's warm, salty skin.

Medea, there are things called crayons.
They are smooth like chalk,
waxy like a candle,
and they leave colorful streaks on paper.
There are things called trampolines
like a fishing net stretched tight
but not for fish—
for jumping, and running around the edge,
and sometimes falling.
and learning new words,
like "ouchie."
There are things called lemons that make my eyes water.
There are things called dog doors, holes in the wall.
It makes my head swim, so much new,
new words, new people, new things,
but I'm still the same old Rebeka.

CHAPTER ELEVEN

O N HER THIRD MORNING IN AUSTIN, REBEKA WENT TO SEE THE
doctor. She packed some toys in her backpack and folded
up a tiny stroller that looked like Danny's, but smaller. It was the
perfect size for the stuffed bear in her backpack. She noticed that
her suitcase stayed in Alayna's room. Maybe that meant she wouldn't
be left with the doctors at the clinic. Maybe she'd come back with
the Davises.

"This appointment is very important," Anna explained in the car.
"The doctor will decide whether or not he can help you."

Rebeka stared out the window and worried. What if the doctor
said he couldn't help? What if he sent her home with her feet still
curled? When they got to the doctor's office, Clay lifted her out of
the car and she hurried up the hot sidewalk, pushing her stuffed
bear in the tiny stroller.

Before she got to the sliding glass doors, they whooshed open and
cold air spilled out of the building. Clay, Meredith, Natalie, Anna,

and Rebeka all hurried inside, out of the sun. Danny was at home with Alayna and the boys.

While Meredith went to talk to someone at the desk, Rebeka found a seat in the waiting room. There was a TV playing cartoons but she didn't understand any of the words. She looked around at all the other kids waiting for appointments. Some were in wheelchairs. One boy couldn't hold up his head. A long string of drool dripped

Rebeka pushing her doll in a stroller into Dell Children's Medical Center of Central Texas.

from his chin. Rebeka stared at the shimmery thread of spit. It reminded her of Papa's fishing line, and the thought of Papa made her stomach flip.

"Rebeka Uh-wee . . . tonz?" said a woman in blue pants and shirt, holding a clipboard.

"That must be you," said Meredith. She stood up and held out her hand. Rebeka swung her arm up to grab it. It was time.

"I'll be taking Rebeka's temperature and blood pressure and weight," the woman said as they followed her to a small room. She put a band on Rebeka's arm that squeezed. Why was it squeezing? Would it stop? Her heart raced as she stared at Anna, wishing she'd explain, but she was talking to Meredith.

The woman in blue smiled and took off the band. Then she asked Rebeka to stand on a metal platform. It was cold on the tops of her feet and hard to balance. Red numbers blinked on a little screen, and the lady wrote them down.

"Now, sit here, please, and I'll take your temperature."

Rebeka didn't know what she was saying, but she sat down because her legs were trembling. When Anna told her to open her mouth and the woman put a stick under her tongue, she felt a tear trickle down her cheek. She was so afraid of what might come next. Would they do the things that hurt, like at the clinic in Rwanda? Would they give her shots? Would they twist her foot all the way around and hold it in a cast? Would Meredith and Clay leave her here?

"Hey," said Clay. He knelt down and looked into her eyes. "It's okay. Don't be afraid. It doesn't hurt."

Anna translated and Rebeka nodded her head. She knew this didn't hurt. She was worried about later.

"All done," said the woman as she took the thermometer out of Rebeka's mouth. Rebeka bent down and wiped the tear off her cheek.

"Follow me," said the woman. They went down a long hall and into a room with windows. The floors were hard and shiny. Rebeka's black sandals made a squeaking noise each time she took a step. In the room, Clay picked her up and set her on a padded table covered in a long piece of paper. A woman in green pants and a matching green shirt came in.

"My name is Gina," she said. "I'm a registered nurse and I help Dr. Dehne."

Rebeka didn't understand much, but she liked the lady's smile.

"Can I take pictures of your feet?" she asked, and held up a phone.

"She wants to take pictures," Anna explained in Kinyarwanda. Rebeka nodded, and the woman named Gina began to take pictures. Rebeka wished she could hold the phone and take them herself. Alayna had let her use her phone and she had taken hundreds of photos of the dogs and the house and the lake and everything.

The grown-ups chatted as they waited for the doctor. Nobody seemed like they were worried. Maybe it was going to be okay. Maybe nothing would hurt. Rebeka tore off a tiny piece of paper from under her leg and twisted it into a sharp little point. She poked it on her knee, her finger, and inside her stuffed bear's ears.

"Hello!" A tall man with gray hair and glasses strode into the room. He was wearing a pair of light blue pants and a shirt the same color. He smiled a big smile. "I'm Dr. Dehne, and you must be Rebeka!"

Doc tor daynuh. She wished she could understand all his words. He talked fast and moved fast, but he was gentle when he unlaced her shoes and then took her feet and carefully examined them, rubbing the calluses on the top. He looked at her shoulders and arms and hands, too. He even brought in another doctor to look at her arms and shoulders some more. Finally, he turned and talked to the grown-ups for a long time. Rebeka waited for Anna to explain what he was saying. She watched their faces, trying to guess. It was hard to tell. There were worried eyebrows, frowns, and then timid smiles.

Anna finally turned to her and translated. "He's telling us that sometimes, babies who are born with feet like yours are given a series of casts, once a week. Because they are babies, their bones are soft, and after just a few months, their feet turn."

"Oh," said Rebeka. Had her only chance at normal feet come when she was born, or could Dr. Dehne do something about it?

Anna continued. "He isn't sure if casts will work now, since you are older and your bones have gotten used to being twisted after so many years."

"What about my arms? Can he make them stronger so I can lift them?"

Anna shook her head. "I'm sorry, Rebeka. He doesn't think there is anything they can do for your arms."

Hope leaked out of her like a tire going flat. They were going to send her back to Rwanda without doing anything. Dr. Dehne started to talk again and Anna translated.

"He wants to see you walk down the hall."

Clay helped her off the table. She stood up tall and walked her very best for Dr. Dehne. *Chance comes once* was what Papa said, but she was being given a second chance. It was like a gift, so she must do her very best. She moved fast, her arms swinging as she swayed from side to side. *Please God*, she prayed in her head. *Please help me.*

Dr. Dehne rubbed his eyes and scratched his head. Then he said something to Anna.

"They want to take some pictures of your bones," she explained. "We need to go with the nurse."

"My bones?"

"Don't worry, the pictures won't hurt."

How would it not hurt, to slice her skin to the bone to take pictures? She followed Meredith and Anna and the X-ray technician down the hall and trembled as they entered a cold room. It was empty except for a giant machine in the middle. Anna and Meredith helped her put on a hospital gown that tied at the neck and hung open down the back. Her skin prickled with chill bumps. The technician hung a heavy apron over her chest and showed her where to sit and then pressed a piece of smooth, cold glass on the machine to her leg.

"You must hold very, very still or the pictures won't work. Dr. Dehne needs good pictures to decide whether he can help."

"When will they cut?" Rebeka asked Anna.

"Cut?"

"Yes. When will they cut my skin to get to my bones?"

"No! Oh, Rebeka, I'm sorry," said Anna. "We would never do surgery without telling you first! The pictures are taken through your skin. It won't hurt one bit."

The technician said something and then all three of them stepped out of the room.

"We'll be right back," said Anna.

Why did they leave? She held her breath to stop shaking. She thought about home and plates of rice and beans and the warm cooking fire and paper snowflakes dangling from the ceiling, anything to distract her from the cold room and the big, scary machine. The machine beeped.

"Good job!" said the technician as she came back in the room, and Anna translated.

"Thank you," said Rebeka. That was it? A little beep?

The technician put her in a different position and they took more pictures, again and again, at least a dozen times, until finally they were done.

"Now we just have to wait and see what Dr. Dehne says," said Anna.

As they walked back out into the sunshine, Rebeka felt worry, heavy like a lead apron, settling on her shoulders.

What would Dr. Dehne see on her X-rays?

Were her bones right for treatment, or would she go back to crawling someday?

> *Medea,*
> *If anyone wants to take pictures of your bones,*
> *don't worry.*
> *The hardest part is*
> *the waiting,*
> *wondering what will happen next.*
> *If the doctor says no,*
> *if I have to come home with my feet still twisted,*
> *it will hurt at first.*
> *But when I see you,*
> *maybe the hurt will melt*
> *like a crayon*
> *in the hot Texas sun.*

CHAPTER TWELVE

THE NEXT MORNING, WHILE REBEKA WAS LOOKING FOR SHELLS at the edge of the lake, Anna hurried across the backyard.

"Dr. Dehne called! He wants to put a cast on your left foot!"

Rebeka ran across the backyard on the tops of her bare feet, the thick grass soft and cool in the morning air. "When? Today?"

Anna laughed. "No, not today. It will be next week, after Danny and I leave."

"A whole week?" A week felt like a long, long time.

"It will be here before you know it. Dr. Dehne explained that he'll start with your left foot. Every week you'll get a new cast, and with each one he'll turn your foot a little bit more. After three or four casts, he'll know whether it's working. If it is, he'll keep putting on new casts until your foot is ready for surgery."

Rebeka squeezed the shell she was holding, feeling its sharp edges dig into her palm. "How long before surgery?"

Anna put a hand on Rebeka's smooth, shiny head. "Months."

Rebeka looked down at her curled feet, dusted with sand. "Will surgery hurt?"

"You won't feel a thing. You'll be asleep. Besides, that's a long way off. Don't worry about it. Go find some more shells."

The week went faster than she thought, just like Anna said it would. She founds lots of shells and went on boat rides and met new friends on the street who brought her gifts and stayed to play. In Rwanda she was just Rebeka with the twisted feet, but here, everyone wanted to meet her. She ran around and around the edges of the trampoline, or sat in the middle and let someone bounce her instead.

She took trips to the grocery store, where the rows and rows of food took her breath away. There was so much of it that could be had without planting or weeding or watering or harvesting. And then there were other stores, ones with clothes and toys and shoes and dishes. Alayna bought her a tutu with stiff tulle that stuck straight out like she was doing a permanent twirl.

She went to church and Nate held her during the songs so she could see the band play and the singers sing. She even went to the dentist, where there were tiny sharp tools and a strange straw that sucked all the wetness out of her mouth. She didn't like it, but she did like the small, bouncy ball she got when she was done.

Rebeka on a trampoline behind the Davis house.

One evening, Anna sat down next to her. "Rebeka, Meredith wants me to explain something to you before I leave," she said. "The Davises have another home across town that they live in when school starts. You'll be moving soon."

Rebeka nodded and smiled. "Okay."

"Okay?" asked Meredith.

"Okay." She had left her family and her home and flown all the way across the ocean. She was filled up with plenty of food, warm summer days, new friends, and exciting boat rides. She would miss the lake, but moving was going to be okay. She helped fill boxes and pack. She said goodbye to her new friends on the street and took one last boat ride. Too soon, the day came when it was time to say goodbye to Anna and Danny.

"You are going to do just fine," said Anna as she leaned down to hug Rebeka. "You are a brave, strong girl. I will be praying for you."

"Thank you, Anna," said Rebeka, in English, not Kinyarwanda. She grabbed Danny's little hand and gave it a squeeze. She would miss him at the dinner table, laughing with his mouth full of mushy food. "Goodbye, Danny. I love you."

Rebeka uses Alayna's phone to take pictures.

The next morning, Rebeka tried to help the Davises pack up their cars, even though she could carry only light things. They had to move clothes and food, the dogs and Benji's hermit crabs, the picture of Rebeka's family, stacks and stacks of books, and her tutu. She took pictures of everything with Alayna's phone so she wouldn't forget the place that had just begun to feel like a home.

The new house didn't have a lake in the backyard, but there was a big football field on the other side of the back fence with nice, soft grass. In the garage, there was a bicycle with a little seat on the back so Clay could give her rides.

She learned a new word, "more," so she could ask Clay to take her for more and more rides. At least eight kids knocked on the door that first afternoon, friends of Alayna, Nate, and Benji. Soon they were her friends, too. She went to the Rices' house, her sponsor family, on Sunday after church and spent the afternoon baking and

Clay gives Rebeka a bike ride at the house near the school.

playing games. Their house was crowded with kids and clean laundry and good smells.

Finally, it was the morning when she'd get her cast. She was nervous. She kept thinking about when she was three and the doctors at the hospital in Rwanda twisted her leg so hard she cried, and then held it in a cast for a week. And when she was four and she was left alone at the clinic. No amount of twisting and rubbing could make her feet turn then. What if these casts didn't work, either? And what if it hurt?

When they got to the office, Gina took pictures of her feet again and then Dr. Dehne sat on a stool and studied her left foot carefully. He turned it gently this way and that, looking at it from all angles. Beside him was a bowl full of water and a roll of bandages. Panic bubbled up in Rebeka. Anna said it wouldn't hurt, but what did Anna know? She and Danny were far away. She trembled and her eyes filled with tears.

Dr. Dehne was gentle. First he slipped a strange brown sock on her foot and leg. It was soft and very stretchy. Someone had cut out the part that would cover her toes. Next, he wrapped wet bandages around and around and around her foot. The bandages dried quickly and began to harden. Just before the cast hardened completely, Dr. Dehne turned her foot, just a little, and held it until the cast was rigid.

Rebeka couldn't stop shaking, couldn't stop the tears rolling down her cheeks. She was nine years old, in a doctor's office with nobody who could speak her language. The cast felt strange. Her foot was sore, but she couldn't turn it back to where it was comfortable.

She stared at her new cast. It looked like a white sock, but it was hard and heavy.

"How does it feel?" asked Meredith, pointing to her cast with worried eyebrows.

"Ouchie," she said. There was a dull ache near her ankle. "Ouchie," she said again.

"I'm sorry," said Meredith. The word "sorry" felt nice, like Mama's hug or Papa wiping her tears. By the time they got home, her foot had gotten used to the new position and her belly was full of the delicious french fries they'd gotten on the way back. French fries went along with "sorry." They weren't as good as Mama's hug, but they were nice, too.

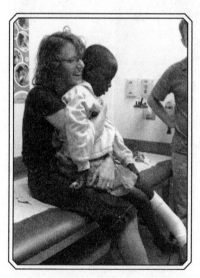

Meredith holding Rebeka on the table in the exam room.

"It looks okay," Alayna said when she saw the cast. "But it's missing something." She took out a red marker and gently moved Rebeka's casted foot across her lap.

"What?" asked Rebeka as she stared at the marker.

Alayna touched the red tip to the white and wrote a word. "Alayna," she said, pointing to her name. "Here, your turn."

Alayna held out the box of markers to Rebeka. She grabbed a blue one and wrote her name, even bigger. Clay wrote his name next, then Meredith, Benji, and Nate. Every time a new friend came over, they also signed her cast.

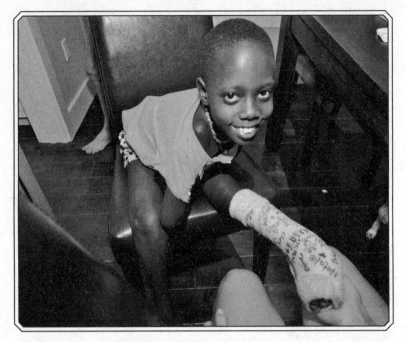

Rebeka's cast filled with signatures.

It was beautiful with the rainbow-colored names, so beautiful Rebeka was almost sad that she'd be getting a new cast in just a week. But she couldn't wait to see what her new foot would look like, and the only way that could happen was taking off her rainbow cast. Everyone would just have to come back and sign the next one, too.

Medea,
I got a cast today.
Everyone signed it except one very important person.
It makes me sad
to see the blank space and remember,
my sister's name is missing.

CHAPTER THIRTEEN

L IFE CHANGED WITH A CAST ON. EVEN THOUGH DR. DEHNE told her she could walk after a few days, she didn't. It hurt to put pressure on her foot, and she was afraid she would lose her balance and fall. She scooted around on the wood floors instead, or let someone carry her. She had not expected to crawl in America. She had come to America so that she would never crawl again.

One afternoon, Meredith took her to the house of a woman named Gayle.

"I'll be back soon," she said. "I just have to go to an appointment. Gayle is my good friend and she is so excited you're here!"

All Rebeka understood was that she had been left. She was sad and afraid. Why couldn't she go with Meredith?

But Gayle was nice. She had cookies and a big dog with silky soft fur and hard wood floors that were perfect for bouncing a ball. A different day, a lady named Jeri came over and took her to lunch. She was another one of Meredith's friends. Rebeka got french fries and Fanta, and they drew pictures with crayons. Jeri liked to kiss her on the cheek, even though she always wiped it off. That just made Jeri laugh. Different kids came by all the time and they played Uno and memory and the days passed until it had been a week since she got her cast. It was so full of names, there was more color than white.

The night before her next appointment, the Davises gathered around her on the floor, chattering like a bunch of birds.

"It's time to take off your cast!" said Meredith.

"What?" asked Rebeka.

Clay drew a picture, but it didn't make any sense. Meredith wrapped toilet paper around her own leg so it looked like a cast, then unwound it. She pointed to Rebeka's left leg. "Dr. Dehne gave you a cast that we can take off at home. He said we can take it off tonight, so you can clean it before tomorrow's appointment!" She pretended to wash her feet and leg, and Rebeka nodded.

"Yes," she said. "Yes. I wash."

Clay started picking at the bandage at the top of her cast, near her knee. She stiffened and winced, but Clay was gentle. Off came the colorful names as the stiff bandage curled in a pile on the floor. It hardly hurt at all, and finally she could see her leg and her foot.

Her skin looked and smelled strange after a week of no washing and sweating under the heavy cast. Rebeka bent closer, examining her foot carefully.

It looked exactly the same.

She blinked back tears.

Anna had said the casts would turn her foot slowly, but it didn't look like it had turned at all.

The Davises didn't seem to notice. They were chatting excitedly, touching her foot and bending down to see it from different angles.

"Let's get you in the bath so you can scrub it clean," said Meredith. She picked up Rebeka and carried her into the bathroom. In the tub, Rebeka explored every bit of her foot, between each toe and all around her ankle. She squinted her eyes and tilted her head. Maybe it did look a little different.

The next day, Dr. Dehne looked at her foot and gave her a thumbs-up, and Gina took more pictures before putting on cast number two. Rebeka wasn't scared a bit this time, and she didn't shed a single tear.

Another week passed. She learned how to stand for short amounts of time, long enough to brush her teeth or wash her hands. It felt good to be upright again, but the days were long since she couldn't play like she did at the lake.

One morning, Alayna, Nate, and Benji came into the kitchen with backpacks slung over their shoulders.

"Goodbye, Rebeka," said Alayna as she walked out the back door. Meredith carried her to the window so they could watch Alayna walk through the gate and across the football field to the school. Benji and Nate followed.

"Goodbye!"

"Goodbye! See you after school!"

She was being left behind again, just like when Medea went to school. She was too old for kindergarten in America, but she didn't know enough to go into fourth grade with all the other nine-year-olds. Besides, she had so many doctor appointments in her future that she would miss a ton of school. Meredith carried her to a chair at the kitchen table and sat down next to her. She picked up a pencil and gave one to Rebeka.

"This is an 'A,'" Meredith said, writing the letter "A" on a piece of paper.

"A," said Rebeka. She knew "A" from her days with chalk on the concrete floor. She gripped her pencil tightly and wrote the letter at the top of her paper.

"Good!" said Meredith. "Very good!"

Rebeka drew another "A," and then another, until the letter "A" went from one edge of the paper to the other. Meredith drew an apple underneath her letter "A." Then she picked up a crayon and colored it red. "A, apple," she said.

What did an apple have to do with school, or homework, or the letter "A"? Rebeka drew an apple, then glanced out the window. It was going to be a long, long day. They drew more "A"s. Then they counted, and did flash cards, and learned a song about the days of the week that she couldn't sing because she didn't know any of the words yet. It was hard to pay attention learning all by herself. After a while, Meredith set out blank paper and crayons and picked up her laptop.

"Are you okay?" she asked Rebeka. "I have to work for a while."

"Okay," said Rebeka. She crawled out of the room, looking for something more exciting than paper and crayons. There was a room between the bedroom she shared with Alayna and the bedroom where Meredith and Clay slept. They called it the "middle room" and it was a mess of things that hadn't been put away yet after the move. The floor was scattered with leftover school supplies and clothes that needed to be put away and pictures that needed to be hung. There were markers and scissors and all sorts of things spread out on the carpet.

She crawled over to Alayna's dresser. They had moved it out of her room to make room for Rebeka's bed. She swung her arm up to the top drawer on the left and pulled it open. It was filled with socks of every color, some long, some short, some without a match. Rebeka imagined how wonderful it would be to someday wear socks on her turned-flat feet.

She sighed and closed the drawer. A metal hook caught her eye. Rebeka crawled across the floor to inspect it closer. The hook was mounted on a square plate, and on the back of the plate was a small loop of metal for hanging. If the hook was on the wall, it would be the perfect place to hang her tutu.

She didn't feel like waiting for someone else to hang it. She was always waiting. Waiting for someone to pick her up, waiting for someone to play, and waiting for her feet to turn, but she didn't have a hammer or nail to hang the hook. She looked around the room and spied a roll of tape. She scooted to it on her bottom and put it around her wrist like a fat bracelet. Then she scooted back to the hook and used her teeth to tear off wide, sticky pieces.

What a wondrous thing this tape was! How Papa would love a roll. She stuck the pieces to the hook and took it over to the wall. Swinging her arms, she got the hook where she wanted it and then leaned against it to hold it in place while she pressed on the piece of tape. Then she scooted back and took a look.

It was perfect.

She picked up her tutu and, swinging her arms again, she managed to catch it on the hook.

Rebeka's tutu hanging on the wall.

"Rebeka, you okay in there?" Meredith called from the other room.

"Okay!" said Rebeka, and giggled. "Meredith! Come!" she called.

"Wow," said Meredith when she came into the room. "Did you do that by yourself?"

Rebeka grinned as Meredith took pictures with her phone of the tutu on the hook. She might not be in fourth grade, but she was smart.

Medea,
Meredith took me to a place
where the ground was covered in tiny rocks
that left chalky prints on my skin.
I sat at the top of a long red plastic tube
and Meredith said let go
and I said no
and she said yes
until I did, and I slid
down to the bottom.
And I climbed back up and did it again and again
and my skin was covered in chalky rock prints.
I also sat on a piece of soft rubber attached to chains
and Meredith pushed on my back

and I swung back and forth
and my stomach felt funny.
The place was called a playground.
I've spent my whole life playing on the ground
but it's never been that fun.

CHAPTER FOURTEEN

REBEKA GOT CAST NUMBER THREE ON HER LEFT FOOT, AND THEN four. Gina showed her the pictures she had been taking at each appointment, and when she scrolled from the very first, Rebeka could tell that her foot really was turning, slowly but surely. She did more school, drawing pictures of balls for "B" and cats for "C" and drums for "D." Meredith taped them to the window, next to her "A" for apple, just as Mama had hung her snowflakes from the ceiling back home for everyone to admire. One morning, a new woman came to their home. She had two big bags on her shoulders, bright eyes, and a wide smile.

"Mrs. Karen used to teach in a school, and she has all sorts of ideas to help you learn," Meredith explained. "I'll be in the kitchen if you need me."

Mrs. Karen sat down next to Rebeka at the dinner table and started pulling things out of one of her bags. "Let's find out what words you know. What is this?" Mrs. Karen asked, pointing to a little bed. It was funny. Who would sleep in such a bed? Why had someone taken the time to make something so tiny and perfect?

"Bed," Rebeka said, her voice almost a whisper. What if it was the wrong word?

"What? I can't hear you!" said Mrs. Karen. She got out of her chair and walked to the other side of the room. "What is it?" she asked, holding up the tiny bed.

"Bed!" said Rebeka, in the voice she used to play with Medea back home, the voice she used when she was zooming on the boat at the lake or running around the edge of the trampoline.

"Good!" Mrs. Karen shouted back.

Rebeka liked Mrs. Karen. She brought bright-colored cubes that linked together for counting, and puzzles and games that felt more like playing than learning. She even made headbands out of color-ful ribbons for her to wear over her slowly growing hair. But Mrs. Karen couldn't bring a class full of kids with her, and Rebeka was still lonely, learning all by herself.

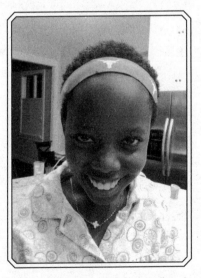

One Friday night, Rebeka saw bright lights over the fence and heard loud music. Clay carried her to the bleachers by the foot-ball field. There were people everywhere. When they glanced her way she watched as they noticed her cast and her twisted

Rebeka wearing one of the headbands Mrs. Karen made.

right foot. Most smiled, several said hello, but some looked away as if they were in trouble for noticing. She held her head high and acted like it was perfectly normal, a nine-year-old girl with dark black skin being carried around like a baby, living with a family of *muzungus*, one foot in a cast and the other curled.

Clay handed her a small bag of candy. She held it carefully so it wouldn't spill, taking out one colorful piece at a time and chewing it slowly to make it last. Girls in matching short skirts jumped and kicked on the sidelines while boys with large shoulders and tight pants threw a brown ball and ran up and down the field. After a while, Alayna and some other girls marched onto the field wearing white boots and sparkly twirly-skirts. They kicked their legs, all their boots in the air at the exact same time.

"Yay, Alayna!" she yelled when everyone else clapped. Her hands made no noise when she tapped them together, but it was the best she could do with her limp arms. She longed to run or kick or cheer instead of sitting on the hard metal bench.

Behind the bleachers, kids laughed and talked and chased one another in the grass. Papa's words echoed in her head: *Chance comes once.* She may not be able to play football or cheer on the sidelines, but this was her chance to make a friend. She nudged Meredith and pointed to the ground with her chin, raising her eyebrows and staring intently. "I go?" she asked.

"Hmmm," said Meredith. "It's kind of crazy down there."

"It's okay," said Rebeka.

So Clay laid a blanket on the ground next to the bleachers for her. "You sure you'll be okay?" he asked.

"Go," said Rebeka, pointing to the bleachers with her chin.

"Okay, okay. I'll keep an eye on you from there."

A little boy plopped down on her blanket. He looked about Medea's age. He stared at her cast and said some things she couldn't understand, then held out a football. She shrugged her shoulder to grab it with both hands and tried to toss it back to him, but it was hard to get her arm swinging while she was sitting down. The ball fell on the blanket. The boy grabbed it and got back up to run with his friend.

More kids stopped and said hello. Rebeka smiled her best smile, but she didn't have enough words to make them stay. After a while, a girl with straight brown hair, a round face, and tiny freckles dotting her white skin sat down.

"Hi, I'm Kate," she said.

"My name is Rebeka." Rebeka picked at a loose thread on the blanket. She waited for Kate to get up and run off, but she didn't.

"How old are you?" Kate asked.

Rebeka knew this question. Mrs. Karen had taught her. "I am nine years old," she said carefully, making sure she said her words just right.

"I'm ten."

"My birthday is September twentieth," she said, slowly and clearly. Each day she put an "X" on Meredith's calendar, marking out another day. Her birthday was only a few days away now.

"Wow, that's soon!" said Kate.

Rebeka smiled and nodded, even though she wasn't sure what the words meant. She was pretty out of words she knew. Now what?

"I heard you are from Rwanda," Kate said.

Rebeka heard the word "Rwanda" and nodded.

"We adopted my little brother from there."

Just then, a little boy dashed past with a shoe tucked under his arm like a football. His skin was a deep, dark brown, just like Rebeka's.

"Cooper!" Kate called. "Come say hi."

Cooper didn't stop. Kate rolled her eyes at Rebeka and said, "Boys!"

Rebeka rolled her eyes, too. "Boys!" she repeated, and giggled. She knew the word "boys." Nate and Benji, they were boys.

She stayed on the blanket with Kate for a long time, until the football game was over and the big lights above the field turned off. *Maybe someday I will run with Kate across that field*, she thought.

Rebeka and Kate with french fry "mustaches."

After that day, Kate came by often, and on Rebeka's birthday they went out for french fries. Kate pinched a french fry between her top lip and her nose and Rebeka did the same.

"It's a mustache," said Kate.

"Mustache," repeated Rebeka. The french fry fell off when she started laughing. It wasn't until that night, when it was dark and quiet and she was trying to get comfortable in her heavy cast, she remembered Medea and home. She wondered if they remembered that today was her special day.

Medea,
There is a bell that sits beside my bed
that I ring if I have to go to the bathroom
in the middle of the night.
Meredith or Alayna carry me to the toilet.
I can't get on it by myself with this cast on my foot.
A ten-year-old girl
(that's right, I'm ten now!)
should not have to announce
that she needs to go to the bathroom.
I know it is a small thing,
compared with all the other things.
But lying here, in this quiet house,
I do not want to ring the bell.

CHAPTER FIFTEEN

A T HER FOURTH CAST-CHANGE APPOINTMENT, DR. DEHNE DREW an imaginary line on the back of her ankle. "Your tendon is stretching nicely and the casts are working. It's time to schedule surgery! I'll make an incision here and cut the tendon, then set it in place with a cast that will hold it there for several weeks."

Rebeka didn't understand a lot of what he said, but she understood the words "surgery" and "cut." She cut paper snowflakes with scissors. Dr. Dehne would cut her skin.

"How about November fifth?" asked Dr. Dehne.

"Sounds great," said Meredith. "I'll put it on our calendar."

Dr. Dehne put a long cast on her left leg, and a short cast on her right leg so it would start turning, too. The bottom half of her body felt so heavy. Moving around was even harder, and both her legs had a dull ache. Now that surgery was actually going to happen, she felt the way she did when Mama was about to pour cold water on her head to wash the soap off her body. She couldn't wait to get it over with.

They visited a special nurse at the hospital who asked her what smells she liked best. She held several bottles under Rebeka's nose. There was no mango smell, no Mama smell or cooking chicken smell, but orange would do. It reminded her a little of orange Fanta. The nurse squirted the scent into a plastic mask that she held over Rebeka's nose and mouth.

"When it's time for surgery," said the nurse, "you'll smell the good orange smell and then you'll go to sleep."

She also sent home a plastic container divided into sections. Each section had a different kind of candy. There were tiny sprinkles, mini chocolate chips, Tic Tacs, M&M'S, and the biggest candy, jelly beans.

"You'll need to be able to swallow pills after surgery, and your pain pill will be this big," said Meredith, pointing to a jelly bean. Rebeka nodded. She watched Meredith carefully, trying to understand. "We'll start with something small to practice." She picked up a sprinkle. "Don't chew it, just swallow." Meredith put it in her mouth, held it on her tongue, then took a drink and swallowed.

Rebeka picked up a sprinkle and swallowed it, no problem. She picked up a jelly bean next.

"Are you sure?" asked Meredith. "Those are pretty big."

Rebeka put it on her tongue and swallowed.

"Good, Rebeka. You're going to do great!"

One afternoon she went with Alayna, Nate, and Benji to a place where pumpkins covered a big lawn. They each picked out their favorite, and when they got back home, Alayna helped her draw a face on the side of her pumpkin. Then Nate helped her slice through the orange flesh and scoop out the slimy insides. She thought about surgery, about the knife cutting her skin and what she might look like inside. She shook her head and concentrated on carving her pumpkin with her favorite silly face, one eye big and one eye small.

Alayna explained about knocking on doors and saying "trick or treat" and getting candy, but none of Halloween made much sense to her. That was okay. She liked candy.

Halloween morning, after Alayna, Nate, and Benji left for school, Meredith said, "I have a surprise. You get to talk to your parents this morning! Someone from Africa New Life is bringing them to the office in Kigali so they can use the computer!"

"What?"

Rebeka making a silly face with her carved pumpkin.

"Your mama and papa, on the computer!" Meredith pointed to her laptop and to the framed picture of her family.

"Mama? Papa?"

"That's right! You get to see them and talk to them!" Meredith held her hand up to her ear like a telephone.

Rebeka's stomach fluttered. It had been almost two months since she'd talked to her parents.

"Sit right here and I'll hook the call up to my laptop."

Rebeka sat at the kitchen table and waited. Suddenly, her parents appeared on the screen. They were sitting at a table and Mama had on her best dress. They smiled and waved.

"*Muraho*, Rebeka, *mwaramutse*!" they said.

Hello. Good morning. Their voices, her language, all that was home and familiar came rushing back to Rebeka in a flood of memory. "*Muraho*," she said. Her parents leaned forward.

"Talk louder," said Meredith. "They can't hear you."

"*Amakuru?*" her father asked.

How was she? She was suddenly filled with longing for home. Her eyes swam with tears and she couldn't speak. Silent tears slid down her cheeks.

"Rebeka, say something to your parents," Meredith whispered. "They need to know you're okay."

She was not okay.

"*Wihangane*, Rebeka," said her mother.

Rebeka nodded her head. Mama's sympathy only made her want to cry more.

"*Ndagukunda,*" said her mother.

"I love you, too," said Rebeka in English, and felt like a traitor.

English came easier than Kinyarwanda now. "*Ndagukunda*," she said. The syllables felt funny in her mouth. Her worlds swam together in a blur of tears.

Meredith handed her tissues and rubbed her back as she told her parents about the surgery. A translator listened and then repeated what she said in Kinyarwanda, while Rebeka listened and tried not to cry.

Finally, her parents called "*Murabeho!*" and waved goodbye.

"Goodbye," Rebeka whispered.

Once the screen went blank, Meredith picked her up from the chair and set her on the couch. She cried some more. She felt undone inside, filled with regret. It had been her one chance to talk to her parents, and she had cried the whole time. Maybe she'd get another chance, the way she'd gotten another chance to turn her feet straight with Dr. Dehne, after not getting surgery as a baby. *Chance comes once* helped her be brave and do hard things, but she could always hope for a second chance.

"I'm sorry that made you so sad," said Meredith.

Rebeka leaned into Meredith's side, taking comfort in her warmth. They sat there a long time, until gradually, her tears dried up and her breath became even again. Molly jumped up and licked her arm.

"Molly, stop!" Rebeka said, but she didn't push her away. She tangled her fingers in Molly's white fur, rubbed her warm body, and felt a little better.

When it started getting dark that night, she helped Clay light candles to set inside their carved pumpkins. Alayna slipped a black headband with plastic mouse ears over Rebeka's head and fluffed her shiny dress over her legs. She sat in a jog stroller that was easier to push than her wheelchair.

"You are the cutest Minnie Mouse ever!" she said.

The street was filled with kids in costumes. Everyone looked different and strange, but nothing was stranger than a ten-year-old girl wearing a pink shiny dress and mouse ears, both legs in casts, being pushed in a stroller. She got the most stares, but she also got the most candy, so it was okay. She was used to stares, and the costumes and candy helped her forget her

Alayna and Rebeka dressed up for Halloween trick-or-treating.

afternoon tears until it was time for bed and all was quiet again.

> *Medea,*
> *Tell Mama and Papa I'm just fine.*
> *I know I was crying, but I'm fine.*
> *I'm ready for surgery.*
> *I can swallow a jelly bean whole.*
> *And all I have to do is smell the orange smell*
> *and fall asleep*
> *and when I wake up,*
> *my left foot will be as straight as yours.*
> *I'll be able to walk and run just like you*
> *. . .*
> *maybe faster.*

CHAPTER SIXTEEN

THE MORNING OF HER SURGERY, MEREDITH woke REBEKA UP very early. Alayna whispered goodbye and fell back asleep. It was still dark outside as Clay drove down the highway and Meredith reminded her all about the orange smell and falling asleep before surgery. She hugged her Curious George stuffed monkey and squeezed Tiny Baby's hand. *Curious George* was her favorite show because George didn't talk. He just squeaked. She could understand him just as much as anyone else. And she had found Tiny Baby at the back of the toy closet her first day at the lake house. She was just a doll, but it was still comforting to hold her tiny hand, and she liked that she could pick this baby up and hold her and take care of her. Not like a real baby.

When they got to the hospital, Clay pushed her wheelchair through the double glass sliding doors. It was cold inside. Rebeka shivered as Meredith talked to a woman at a desk. This was different from the office where she usually saw Dr. Dehne and Gina.

When Meredith was done, she came and sat next to Clay, facing Rebeka's wheelchair.

"Now we just have to wait for the nurse to come get us," she said.

Rebeka nodded but didn't say anything. She chewed her bottom lip and picked at her middle finger, pulling it and letting it snap back to her palm. Would she be able to see the cut Dr. Dehne made in her skin? How bad would it hurt? Suddenly, she felt Tiny Baby pulled out of her hand.

"Clay!" Rebeka told him sternly. "Give her back!"

"What? I don't have Tiny Baby!" he said. He looked for her under his chair and in the pockets of his jacket, and then finally he rocked to one side, pulled her out from underneath him, and gave her back to Rebeka.

"You no sit on Tiny Baby!" she scolded him. When he tried to steal her again, she twisted away to keep her baby safe.

"Rebeka Uwitonze?"

It was a nurse, calling her name.

"Let's go!" said Meredith. She got up and pushed Rebeka's wheel-chair, while Clay followed, carrying her bags. She was still trying so hard not to laugh at Clay that it pushed aside her worries and fears, at least for a moment.

Just past the waiting room, the nurse handed her a pair of special pajamas. Meredith helped her put them on. They looked kind of like the clothes Dr. Dehne wore. She also put a plastic bracelet on Rebeka's wrist with her name typed on it. They went to a small room with a bed in the middle and a couple of chairs. Clay lifted her out of her wheelchair and into the bed. Her stomach did a flip-flop.

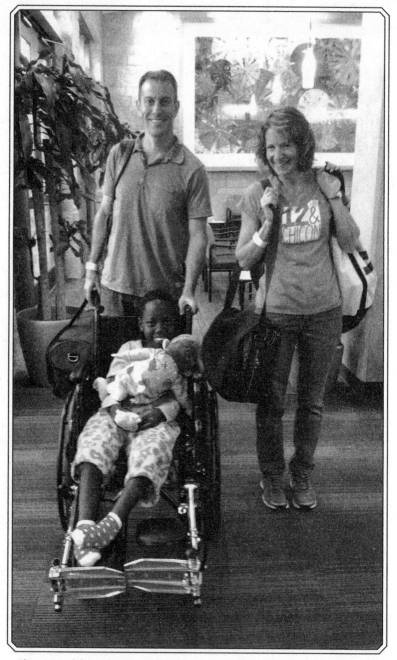

Clay, Meredith, and Rebeka at Dell Children's Medical Center the morning of Rebeka's first surgery.

There were machines and tubes all around their little room. A nurse drew an "X" on her left ankle with a big black marker.

"This is so Dr. Dehne will operate on the correct foot," he said, and Clay and Meredith laughed.

Rebeka touched the big black X and frowned. It was on her skin, not a cast. What if it didn't wash off?

Another nurse came in. "Are you ready, Rebeka?" she asked.

Chance comes once. This was why she came to America. She may never again have the chance for surgery, the chance to walk on the bottom of her turned-straight feet. And still, she wasn't sure she was ready.

The nurse pushed some levers to unlock the wheels on her bed, and Meredith and Clay stood up as she pushed the bed out of the room. Rebeka squeezed Curious George very tight as she rolled down a long hall.

"We can't go past those doors," said Meredith, walking alongside the bed and pointing. "But don't worry, don't be afraid, Rebeka. Remember, they'll put the mask on your nose and it will smell like oranges and then you'll fall asleep."

She didn't want to fall asleep.

What if she didn't wake up?

The nurse stopped the bed. Meredith leaned down and kissed Rebeka's cheek and so did Clay. She didn't shrug the kisses off this time. She let them stay on her cheek.

"Don't worry. You'll be fine," Clay said. "We love you."

A tear trickled out and fell into her ear.

She did not want to go alone, she did not want to smell oranges and fall asleep, but the nurse kept pushing her bed and she couldn't see Meredith and Clay anymore and all of a sudden she was in a big room with bright lights and she thought she could see Dr. Dehne but he had a green mask over his nose and mouth so she couldn't be sure.

Everyone was wearing masks over their noses and mouths.

Like Halloween.

Only scarier.

A nurse stood over her with a plastic mask attached to a hose. It was making a hissing sound. She shook her head, no, no, no, as the nurse held the mask over her nose and she was drowning in oranges, so many oranges . . .

Medea?
Medea?
I'm so
so
sleepy . . .

CHAPTER SEVENTEEN

W HEN SHE WOKE UP, SHE WAS LYING IN A BED IN A LARGE room. Her head felt funny. It was hard to think. There were two clear tubes taped to her arm. The tubes trailed up to a silver pole beside her bed, with bags hanging from it. She couldn't feel her left leg. And her foot . . . did the surgery work?

She lifted her head, thinking she would sit up and try to stand, but she immediately felt dizzy and lay back down. She looked around the room with her eyes only, not wanting to move her head again. There was a curtain on either side of her, and across the room was another bed with a little girl in it. A woman was holding her hand.

Where were Clay and Meredith? Panic rose up inside her. They had left her here. She was all alone.

A nurse hurried over. "Your parents are on the way. They've been talking to Dr. Dehne and they'll be here in just a second."

Her parents? Mama and Papa? She was too tired and foggy to try to figure out all the words.

"Rebeka? Hey, we're right here." Meredith and Clay came around the curtain and hurried to her side. "You look great! How do you feel?"

"My leg," she said. "No feel my leg."

"It's okay. It's just the medicine," said Meredith. "Dr. Dehne said the surgery went well."

"Good?" asked Rebeka.

"Good," said Meredith. She pulled the sheet off Rebeka's leg so she could see.

What she saw was another cast, but it was in the shape of a normal, turned-straight foot. If she stood up, the bottom of her cast would be flat on the ground.

Someone on the other side of her curtain started to cry. Farther away, a child moaned as though he was in pain. Rebeka felt like joining the chorus, felt like wailing for Mama and home and all that was familiar in this room filled with strangers. A sob heaved through her chest and caught in her throat, like a hiccup. Meredith grabbed her hand, and she squeezed it tight.

"You want to watch *Curious George*?" asked Clay.

"Yes," she said. "Yes, please." She wanted to escape this room. He set his computer on her lap and slid a pair of pink headphones over her ears. They had soft padding that muffled the noises in the big room. All she heard were George's squeaks and the happy music of her favorite show, and she felt like she could breathe again.

It wasn't long before they wheeled her bed to a different little room with no other children. When nobody was looking, she picked at the tape on her arm and peeled it back enough to see a needle poking into her skin. She quickly replaced the tape and tried not to think about it. She hated needles.

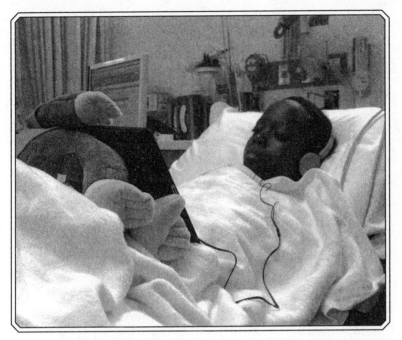

Rebeka in bed with headphones on after her first surgery.

Visitors brought balloons and gifts and it was almost like a party, but then the pain medicine wore off and her foot started to hurt. Meredith showed her how to press a button so that medicine would go from the bag on the pole, down the clear tube, and into her body. Each time she pressed the button, she felt the pain go away and her body relaxed.

It was a long night. Nurses came in five times, waking her up to put a squeezy thing on her arm, and take her temperature, and check the bags on her silver pole. When she had to go to the bathroom, Meredith carried her, making sure all the tubes were out of the way and rolling the pole so she stayed connected to the pain medicine.

The next morning, Dr. Dehne came and checked on her. "You look good, and the surgery went really well. I'm sending a doctor who will give you some special medicine to take with you, and then you can go home."

Meredith packed their things, and she drifted in and out of sleep while they waited for the doctor with his special medicine. When he came, he inserted a tiny tube into her back, near her waist. She didn't feel much when he put it in, just a pinch. The thin tubing led to a plastic ball that was inside a bag. The bag had a strap so she could wear it across her chest like a purse.

"There's pain medicine in this ball," said the doctor. "It should last for several days. When the ball is empty, Meredith can just pull out the tube."

It was good to come home. The balloons her friends brought hung

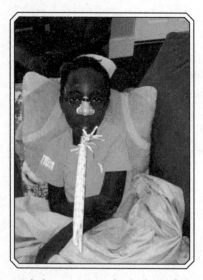

Rebeka trying to make the best of it after surgery.

from the ceiling of the living room, their curled strings like long, colorful hair. Kate brought her some funny glasses and a toy horn. When she blew, it made a noise and a curled piece of paper straightened out. She liked the toy, and she loved Kate, but she didn't feel much like playing. She really didn't feel good.

She watched a movie on the couch about a princess who wore fancy dresses and danced in little slippers. She kept falling asleep and waking up at different parts of the movie, until she finally just turned it off and rolled over.

At bedtime she propped her foot up on a couple of pillows and set her ball full of medicine on the floor beside her bed.

"Mom," said Alayna. "You go to bed. I'll get Rebeka if she needs to go to the bathroom tonight."

"Are you sure?"

"I'm sure. I'll read to her, too."

So Meredith went to her room to go to sleep and Alayna read Rebeka a book. She drifted off to sleep and woke up minutes or hours later, feeling hazy. The house was very quiet. Everyone must be sleeping. She tried to roll over and remembered she was connected to the ball full of medicine. She reached down to scratch her leg and realized her nightgown and underwear were all wet.

"Alayna!"

Alayna sat straight up.

"Rebeka?" She rubbed her eyes. "Do you need to go to the bathroom?"

"I'm wet," Rebeka said.

"Oh no!" Alayna carried Rebeka to the bathroom and changed the sheets on her bed. Once she was all clean and dry with a fresh set of pajamas, she lay back down. She fell asleep but then woke up a little later, soaking wet again. This time her foot hurt. It throbbed like a drum.

"Alayna!"

Alayna woke up, and they did the whole thing over again; clean sheets, clean pajamas, back to bed. "My foot is ouchie," she said, tears pricking her eyes.

"I'm sorry," said Alayna. She yawned and rubbed her eyes. "Let's prop your foot up more."

When she woke up a third time, she was crying as she woke up Alayna.

"There is no way this is pee," said Alayna as she smelled the sheets. She carried Rebeka to the bathroom and sat her on the toilet. "Hold on, I'll go get Mom."

She was hurting and tired and miserable. After a few minutes, Meredith hurried into the bathroom.

"I think your pain medicine must be leaking out of the tube in your back," she said. She checked the tube, pushing it in more firmly and taping it down so it wouldn't get pulled loose. Then she gave her a pain pill the size of a jelly bean. "Swallow this. It will help you feel better."

Rebeka swallowed it and they all went back to bed, but she wasn't tired. "Alayna?" she asked.

"Yeah?"

"It's ouchie."

Alayna sighed. "I'm sorry, Rebeka. I wish I could do something to help you. Your medicine will work soon. Here, this will distract you from the pain."

She handed Rebeka a toy. Rebeka pushed the button and blue and red lights spun inside a clear plastic globe, making designs on the ceiling.

"Isn't it pretty? Does that help?" asked Alayna.

"A little." She still hurt. A lot.

It wasn't long before Alayna was snoring, but Rebeka stayed up and watched the lights for a long, long time as her foot pounded with pain. At first, she was angry. *If I was in Rwanda, this wouldn't be happening to me. My foot wouldn't hurt, and Medea would be right beside me, and I'd be sleeping right now instead of awake in the middle of the night.*

She watched the colors spin. *But if I was in Rwanda, my feet would still be twisted, and I would have never met the Davises or Kate.*

Her eyelids felt heavy. It was hard to open them again when she blinked. She could feel the pain pill starting to work, making her brain fuzzy and her thoughts clouded. She wondered what Medea was doing right now, and wished she could tell her everything.

Medea?
This medicine makes me feel weird.
Like I'm dreaming, even though I'm awake.
A princess rides
on a purple elephant
with wings
up to the stars
to find her dancing shoes
while a drum beats
a painful rhythm
in my foot.

CHAPTER EIGHTEEN

THE NEXT DAY, MEREDITH PULLED THE TUBE OUT OF HER BACK. She was no longer tethered to the plastic ball of medicine with its hassle of straps and tubes. It didn't hurt to remove it, but it meant she didn't have any more strong pain medicine going straight into her body. Meredith and Clay moved her bed to the middle room between theirs and Alayna's, since she woke up every three hours to take pain pills and Alayna needed her sleep because she woke up early for school. Rebeka almost didn't care that she was sleeping in a room by herself now. She was just ready for her foot to stop hurting.

After a few days, she no longer needed to take the giant jelly bean–sized pain pills.

She started feeling better, even good enough to skateboard down the driveway, but a week after surgery, it was time to go back to the hospital. She didn't want to go back, now that she was finally feeling better.

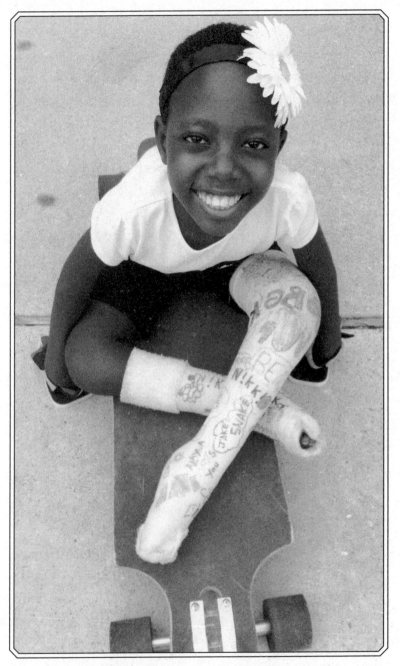

Rebeka on a skateboard on the Davis driveway.

"They need to put you to sleep like when you had surgery, so Dr. Dehne can change your cast," Meredith explained. "He said it would hurt too bad to take off your cast at home, and he needs to take a look at your foot and ankle to make sure everything is healing well."

Meredith spoke slowly. Rebeka still didn't understand everything she said, but she understood enough. She had to go back to the hospital. When they got there, she changed into the pajamas they gave her, and then went into a room with a bed in the middle and machines all around. She was trembling from cold and fear. She remembered being pushed alone through those big swinging doors for surgery, and how scary it was to have the mask put over her nose and mouth.

"Maybe you should hide," said Clay.

"Hide?"

"Yeah. Before the nurse gets here. Bend over and I'll cover you up."

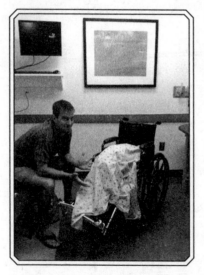
Rebeka hiding under a hospital gown.

Rebeka knew he was just trying to make her laugh, but she bent over anyway and he covered her with a blanket.

"I'm looking for Rebeka Uwitonze. Have you seen her?" she heard a nurse ask.

"No. I have no idea where she is," said Clay. "I think she ran away because she doesn't like that orange smell very much. I'm just going to sit right here."

She could feel Clay beginning to sit on her, his weight pressing down gently. "Hey!" Rebeka yelled.

"Oh, there she is!" he said as she sat up and the blanket fell off. Clay pretended to look surprised and Rebeka started laughing.

"Thank goodness he didn't sit on you!" said the nurse. Then she knelt down and looked in her eyes. "You know, there's medicine we can give you that will help you fall asleep while you're still here with Clay and Meredith, before we give you the orange smell. Would that make it a little easier?"

Rebeka didn't catch all the words. She looked back and forth from Meredith to the nurse. "You want medicine?" Meredith asked Rebeka. "Makes you sleepy? With me?"

"Yes!" Rebeka said. She did have a choice after all, and she didn't want to fall asleep alone.

"I have to warn you, it tastes very bad," said the nurse.

"It's yucky," Meredith explained, making a face.

"It's okay." She didn't want to fall asleep alone to the orange smell again.

The nurse brought a small cup filled with clear medicine. It smelled awful.

"Take it fast," said Clay. "Then you won't taste it." He pretended he was drinking it, throwing back his head and gulping, then wiping his mouth and grinning a giant smile, then rolling his eyes back in his head and slumping in his chair as if he was asleep.

Rebeka threw back her head and drank it all in one swallow. It tasted even worse than it smelled. She opened her mouth and stuck out her tongue. "Uh, uh, uh," she grunted.

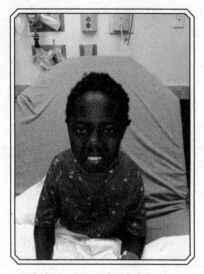

Rebeka making a face after taking
yucky-tasting medicine.

"Here, wipe your tongue on this," said Meredith. She handed Rebeka a paper towel.

She wiped off as much taste as she could, spitting out little bits of paper that stuck to her tongue, and then Meredith carried her to the water fountain so she could drink and spit, drink and spit. A few minutes later, she had trouble opening her eyes when she blinked. She could feel the medicine working, slowing her blinks, her breathing, and her fear. She grinned at the nurse when he came in and fell asleep before they even started wheeling her bed out of the room. Much better.

When she woke up, she was in a lot of pain, way worse than when she woke up from surgery the last time. She hugged her stuffed Curious George tight and tried to watch the movie that played on Clay's computer, but her ankle and foot hurt, hurt, hurt. She squeezed Meredith's hand, and Clay wiped her tears as Dr. Dehne talked.

"Her incision looks great. It's healing really well, but she's going to be pretty sore from the procedure for a couple of days."

Finally, the nurse gave her enough medicine to make it stop hurting so she could go home. Over the next week, the pain got a little bit better each day. She tried to do schoolwork, but it was hard to concentrate. When Kate visited, Rebeka didn't feel like surfing down the driveway on skateboards, or building a fort out of old boxes. She spent a lot of time staring out the window at the leaves that were turning brown and falling off the trees. The weather was growing colder. She wore a jacket when she went outside and stretchy leggings that fit over her casts.

She cheered up a little when they went to the lake for something called Thanksgiving. Everyone was home from school for a few days, and they watched funny movies together, which helped take her mind off her throbbing foot. But she couldn't get in the lake with two casts on, it was too cold anyway, and she couldn't run around the edges of the trampoline, either. Everything felt different from before.

She went to the hospital for cast change number two the day before Thanksgiving. There were pictures of turkeys, drawn by patients, taped to the front desk. Rebeka had never seen such a strange-looking bird. She took more nasty-tasting medicine and had more pain when she woke up. She began to wonder if it was worth it, all the casts and the surgery and the throbbing pain. She just wanted to feel better.

The morning after her second cast change, Clay's parents and grandmother came over. Alayna cleared some space in the middle of the kitchen island so Rebeka could see what was going on and help chop and stir. It was nice to have something to do to take her mind off her foot.

A few hours later, Meredith took a big turkey out of the oven. It didn't look anything like the pictures Rebeka had seen taped to the hospital desk. Alayna put a pan of sweet potatoes dotted with

Rebeka sitting on the kitchen counter, helping to cook the Thanksgiving meal.

marshmallows on the kitchen table. There were three kinds of pies and green beans and a basket full of warm bread. They sat around the big table, Clay said a prayer, and then everyone said, "Happy Thanksgiving," and clinked their glasses together. Nate held Rebeka's wrist up so she could clink, too.

It was good being with family, even if they weren't her family. It felt like it would be forever before she went home. She still needed to have surgery on her right foot, once the cast was done turning her foot. Then she would have to wait until she had no more casts, and then learn how to walk on her new feet.

"We'll come back to the lake for Christmas," Alayna told Rebeka when it was time to go back to the house by the school. "That's just a few more weeks!"

In Rwanda, her family went to church on Christmas Day, and her father killed one of their chickens so they could have a special treat, meat for Christmas dinner, and they would each get a bottle of orange Fanta. At the Davis house, they put a tree in the living room and hung decorations off the branches to get ready for Christmas.

"Christmas morning, there will be presents under the tree," said Alayna. "They'll be wrapped in pretty paper, and you'll get to unwrap them and see what's inside."

Rebeka was excited about Christmas, but there was something

Rebeka hangs ornaments on the Davis Christmas tree.

bigger than presents that she was waiting to unwrap. She couldn't wait to take off her cast at home instead of the hospital, and finally see her brand-new, turned-straight foot.

Medea,
You should have seen Meredith's face
when she saw me using the big knife
to cut sweet potatoes
for Thanksgiving.
I don't know if she thought I was too young,
or if it was too hard for a girl with limp arms
and curled-up fingers
to use a knife like that.
But she didn't take it away, and I cut them all just fine,
and we ate them dotted with marshmallows,
soft and sweet.

CHAPTER NINETEEN

R EBEKA WAS ASLEEP EACH TIME DR. DEHNE CHANGED THE CAST, so she still hadn't seen her foot. She went in for her third cast change, and then her fourth at the hospital. Each week, the pain was a little better when she woke up in the recovery room. Dr. Dehne said it was because her wounds were healing. After the fourth cast change, he smiled and said, "No more operating room for you, Rebeka, not until the surgery on your right foot. We'll leave this cast on for two weeks, and then you can unwrap it at home, like you used to do."

Two weeks was a long time to wait, even when the days were filled with Christmas excitement. Rebeka went caroling on a hay-ride, baked cookies with Kate, and wore a purple satin dress to see the *Nutcracker* ballet. She watched with wide eyes as ballerinas danced and twirled across the stage. Their shoes had laces that wrapped around their ankles, just like Rebeka's old shoes, except their slippers were silk instead of black rubber, and their laces were satin ribbons instead of shoelaces.

Finally, the big day arrived. The entire family gathered around after dinner. As Clay started to pull at the bandage, pain shot through her foot, and her eyes welled up with tears. She jerked back her leg. "Ouchie," she whimpered. "Ouchie."

"Oh, I'm sorry, Rebeka," said Clay. "It's never hurt before."

Her skin felt like a giant bruise, tender and sore, and deeper down she felt stabs of pain, as if someone had crushed up glass and sprinkled it on her bones.

"We can wait," said Clay. "Dr. Dehne can take it off tomorrow in his office."

"No." She shook her head and wiped the tears off her cheeks. She wanted to see her new foot.

"Okay. I'll be careful." Very gently, Clay kept unwrapping her tender foot. He took lots of breaks so she could rest and take a few deep breaths. It hurt worst when he got close to her foot, removing the bandage from her tender skin. She imagined eating a mango, scraping the flesh with her teeth and getting every last bit until the pit was smooth and clean. Her foot was the pit, and once they got to it, there would be no more teeth, no more pain.

Finally, he was done. Rebeka took a deep breath, wiped her cheeks dry on her shoulders, and examined her turned-straight foot carefully. Her heel touched the ground and she felt another stab of pain, so she kept her foot lifted high while she checked out the bulky scar on the back of her ankle and along the outside edge of her foot.

Benji lay on his belly so he could get a good look.

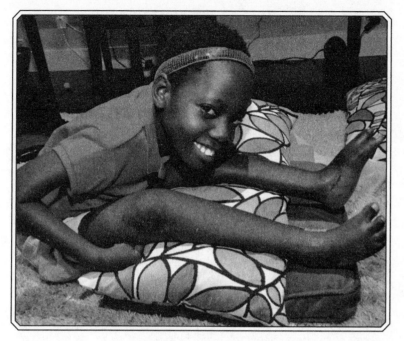

Rebeka's feet with no casts.

"Don't touch," said Rebeka.

"I won't. I'm just looking. It looks good!"

There were dots on either side of the cuts Dr. Dehne had made, where the stitches went in and out to sew her skin together. It didn't look like Medea's pretty foot, the way she imagined it would. It was wider, and scarred from the cuts. But for the first time in her life, her foot was turned so that the bottom of her foot would be flat on the ground.

"It's beautiful, Rebeka," said Meredith. "Dr. Dehne did such a good job."

"But why is it so sensitive?" asked Alayna. "Should we take her to the hospital?"

"No, no, it's okay. Dr. Dehne warned us that her skin might be supersensitive, something about the nerves." Meredith bent down and looked at it closely. "You need a good bath. Maybe your foot will feel better in the water."

"Yes," said Rebeka. She picked at a dry piece of skin on her leg. "I take a bath."

Meredith picked up Rebeka and carried her to the bathroom. She kept her left leg straight and stiff so it didn't touch Meredith's side, and they were very careful going through the doorway so it didn't bump anything. The water felt so nice, and her foot floated so that it didn't touch anything. But how was she going to be able to walk if she couldn't even touch her foot without it hurting?

The next day, Gina smiled wide when she saw Rebeka's foot. "It looks so good!" she said as she took another picture and added it to all the others. She showed Rebeka the picture from her very first appointment.

Rebeka stared at her bent foot, and then at her straight foot. "Wow," she said.

"That's right, wow!"

"It looks great," said Dr. Dehne when he came in, but when he tried to touch it, she pulled away.

"It's really tender," said Meredith. "It hurts when anything touches it."

"That's not unusual. Putting it in a cast is going to hurt, but once it's wrapped, it will feel better."

Rebeka took a deep breath as he wet the bandages, but she couldn't help it. She wailed and screamed as they touched her skin and when Dr. Dehne's hands held the cast in place while it hardened. Clay and

Meredith squeezed her hands and tried to hold her still. They were all trembling when it was over. Her foot felt better now that it was all covered up with the cast, but she didn't look forward to the next time they took it off.

The December days slipped by. They went to the lake house the day before Christmas. She thought about her family at home. She missed them, but it wasn't the sharp pain she felt when she first came to Texas, or when she saw them on Meredith's computer. It was more of a dull ache, like her foot when Dr. Dehne first started putting on casts.

Christmas morning, when Meredith carried her down the stairs, she found a giant surprise under the tree.

Rebeka with a giant Curious George stuffed animal on Christmas morning.

"Georgie!" she squealed.

It was a giant stuffed Curious George, taller than she was when they lay down side by side. Everyone got gifts, some of them wrapped in pretty paper. Benji got a little electric go-kart she couldn't take her eyes off, eager to give it a try. They all went outside to watch him ride it down the long driveway and out into the quiet street. Cars rarely passed the house since the street stopped just a few houses down, but this morning it was even more quiet than usual. Benji zoomed and turned hard to make it skid and slide sideways.

"My turn!" said Rebeka.

"Are you sure?" asked Meredith.

"I'm sure!"

"She can do it," said Clay. "She just needs to be able to squeeze with her hands, and that go-kart is super stable. It's built to drift to the side like that." He put Rebeka on the go-kart seat and helped her prop her casts up. She shrugged her shoulders to get her hands up to the steering wheel.

"Push the thumb trigger on this side to go," said Benji, "and squeeze this bar on the left to stop."

Rebeka pushed the gas trigger on the steering wheel and zoomed off. The speed pressed her back into the seat. She used her shoulders to make her arms turn the wheel, finally in control of when and where and how she moved after being in her casts so long. She turned hard and the go-kart drifted sideways, sliding across the road with a squeal of rubber.

"Rebeka, be careful!" Meredith yelled.

Rebeka threw back her head and laughed. She was free!

At that moment, she didn't care that she was wearing two casts,

Rebeka riding Benji's go-kart on Christmas morning.

and her arms didn't work right, would never work right. She didn't care about the bumpy scar on the back of her ankle or her wider-than-wide feet that hurt to touch. In that moment she was Rebeka, queen of the road. This was the real Rebeka, locked deep inside, waiting for a go-kart to come find her and call her to speed and thrill and freedom.

Medea,
There are things I will never be able to show you.

127

Curious George is too big for a plane,
and so is the little car I can drive
all by myself.
But I will bring home my feet
turned straight,
flat on the ground,
and that's what's most important,
right?

CHAPTER TWENTY

T HE DAY AFTER CHRISTMAS, SHE WENT TO SEE DR. DEHNE SO HE could take off her cast in his office. It hurt a little less after having another week to heal. And a week later when she went in, Dr. Dehne said, "It's time for a brace instead of a cast. You're ready to start learning how to walk again."

"A brace? What is a brace?"

"No more cast!" said Meredith. "A brace is like a hard sock, but you can take it off whenever you want. Now you can learn how to walk!"

"Yes! I can walk and walk and walk," Rebeka said, swinging her feet off the table. She couldn't wait to finally walk, but she wasn't sure how it would happen. Her foot was still supersensitive. Dr. Bud, the brace doctor, came in to make a mold of her foot. He had a white beard and looked a little like Santa, which made her smile, but making the mold hurt. She gritted her teeth until he was through, and she only cried a little.

"Look through these samples and pick the pattern you want for your brace," Dr. Bud said.

Rebeka carefully flipped through all the hard plastic cards. There were tie-dye patterns, dogs, and soccer balls, but she settled on the one with purple butterflies. A week later, they went to Dr. Bud's office to pick up her new brace. It was hard plastic with Velcro straps that fastened around the bottom part of her leg, under her knee. It hurt at first, when her heel touched the hard plastic, but once it was on and the straps were tightened, it didn't hurt anymore. It was like an extra layer of protection between her foot and the rest of the world.

"I want you to wear this brace all the time, even when you're sleeping," said Dr. Bud. "The brace will keep your foot in the correct position, with your ankle at ninety degrees. If you don't wear it, your foot might start to droop, and could eventually curl again."

She listened carefully and nodded. She wasn't sure when or how it happened, but she could understand most of what people said now. Every once in a while, there were words that didn't make sense, but usually she didn't have to guess if she paid close attention.

"I will wear it. I won't take it off," she promised. She would never allow her feet to turn again.

"You can take it off for a bath," said Dr. Bud, "but that's all. And now that you're getting a brace, you'll need some shoes."

"Shoes!" she squealed. Meredith drove straight to the mall when they left their appointment. She pushed Rebeka's wheelchair past store after store. There were so many shoes to choose from, but they needed one that was extra wide so her brace would fit inside. She finally decided on a pair that was bright pink rubber with holes all over them.

Meredith took pictures of Rebeka in her new shoe and sent them to Africa New Life so they could show her parents. She hadn't talked to Mama or Papa since that day they had called and she had cried. She was a little ashamed, and a little afraid it would happen again if they called.

Rebeka in her first shoe after surgery.

Her physical therapist's name was Katie. She was small and strong and full of energy. The first thing Katie did was peel off Rebeka's sock. Her foot felt naked and exposed.

"Feel how soft this brush is," Katie said. She rubbed the brush on Rebeka's palm, and it was soft, but when it touched her toes, it sent a shock of pain through her leg. She jerked her tender foot back, away from the soft plastic bristles.

"You're going to have to brush your foot every day, until it doesn't hurt," Katie said. "I'll send it home with you."

What did brushing her foot have to do with anything? She was ready to start walking and running.

"Don't worry, it won't hurt like this forever. You just have to keep touching it. A lot. It's also important to rub your scars, pressing hard enough to break down all that tough scar tissue." Katie took Rebeka's foot and put her thumb on one of the scars. Rebeka squirmed and tried to pull her foot back.

131

"I'm sorry, but you have to do this if you want to get better." She rubbed tiny circles up and down the bumpy line.

"Ouchie," said Rebeka. "Ouchie!"

Katie patted her knee. "You're a strong girl. You're going to be just fine. Now let's try standing."

Finally. She'd stand, and then walk, and then run across the football field behind the house.

Katie put Rebeka's sock and shoe back on and then held the walker as Rebeka eased up, holding on to the silver bars. She could hardly put any weight on her left foot, and her right foot was still in a cast with her toes pointing straight down so it couldn't take much weight, either. She leaned on the walker, taking her weight on her hands.

"Try to let go of the walker," said Katie.

She leaned back and let go for just a second, lost her balance, and held on again.

"Try again," said Katie. "You need to put more weight on this leg"—she tapped Rebeka's left leg—"so you don't fall."

This reminded her of learning to walk with Medea in the garden. Little by little, Rebeka loosened her grip on her walker. Standing was easier than brushing her foot, but the pressure made it throb. Was she ever going to learn how to walk on her new feet?

"Just keep practicing every day," said Katie, when their appointment was done. "You'll get stronger. Don't give up."

Rebeka took a deep breath as she sat in the wheelchair and Meredith rolled her back to the car. She was tired of trying hard and tired of her foot hurting. She had thought after surgery, when the cast came off, her foot would be all better. She hadn't realized how much work was still ahead of her.

"Are you okay?" Meredith asked from the front seat.

Rebeka didn't answer. She could see Meredith's eyes looking at her in the little mirror.

"Don't worry. It won't be this hard forever. Pretty soon your foot won't be so sore. We just have to keep doing what Katie says." She glanced in the mirror again. "Do you want some french fries?"

"Yes!"

Meredith laughed. "I figured that would make you feel better."

The fries were good, but it felt even nicer to go home and relax. When it was time for dinner, Nate carried her to the table and set her down in her chair. She tapped his arm muscle and said, "You are strong like Clay." She knew so many words now. Having a conversation was easy, nothing like physical therapy.

"No way, I'm stronger than Nate!" said Clay.

"Clay, you are strong like a chicken!" said Rebeka. Everyone laughed.

"How strong am I?" asked Nate.

"Strong like an elephant," she said. Everyone laughed even more. Nate was an elephant. Clay was a chicken.

"Alayna, you are strong like a mouse!"

"Hey!" said Alayna.

"Benji, you are strong like a lizard. Meredith, you are strong like a duck."

"Oh yeah, well, what are you strong like?" asked Clay.

Rebeka looked down at her plastic brace, covered in the purple butterfly print. "I'm strong like a butterfly," she said, and everyone laughed some more.

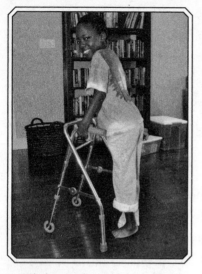

Rebeka standing with her walker.

"Butterflies are actually really strong," said Benji. "The monarch can fly, like, three thousand miles."

"Katie says you're strong, too," said Meredith. "Which reminds me. You need to practice. Why don't you show everyone what you learned?"

"Okay, okay," she said. "I stand one minute." Nate got her walker and she used it to balance.

"I'll start timing as soon as you let go," said Meredith, looking at her watch. "A minute is sixty seconds."

She had learned to count to one hundred with Mrs. Karen. Sixty seconds was a lot of seconds. "Ready, go," said Rebeka, and she let go of the walker.

"Go, Rebeka!"

"You can do it!"

It felt like forever. Her foot throbbed. She grabbed her walker and sat down. "How long?" she asked.

"Fifteen seconds," said Meredith. "But that's okay. It will take a while to work up to one minute. What's important is to keep practicing."

"Yeah, it's okay, Rebeka. A minute is a long time," said Alayna.

Rebeka stared at the table. Practicing was not going to be fun. Meredith wrote down the date and the time on a piece of paper and hung it on the refrigerator. "We'll keep track of how much you stand so we can show Katie."

The column on the piece of paper got longer and longer each day, and each time, she stood a few seconds longer. It wasn't fun, but it felt good to watch her time go up. By the next week, she could stand for a whole minute before sitting down. When Katie saw her practice chart, she was proud.

"Now let's try taking a few steps," she said.

Learning to walk with Katie was different from learning to walk with Medea in the garden. With Medea her legs were weak so she had to build up strength, and she had to learn how to balance, and the tender skin on her feet was sore, but it didn't hurt the way her left foot hurt now. It was like a thousand hard, dried kernels of maize were pricking the bottom of her foot and heel each time she touched it to the ground. But she listened to Katie and she did what she said. When it hurt, she thought about all the years she spent crawling on the ground in Rwanda. She never wanted to do that again. She pushed the walker forward and took baby steps across the room.

Chance comes once. This was her chance to learn to walk again, with the help of Katie and the big physical therapy room at the hospital. She must learn before she went back to red dirt roads and home, where there was no money for fancy hospitals or therapists.

It felt good going forward, but soon it was time to take a few steps back.

She had surgery on her right foot at the end of January. She was back to painful cast changes and waking up in the middle of the night to swallow pain pills. She was back to not feeling like doing anything, her mind foggy with medicine and her right foot throbbing like a drum. The difference was, she had done it before. She knew it didn't last forever.

Kate hung out on the couch and watched movies with her. Rebeka kept doing school when she could, sounding out short words like "pig" and "dog," and adding double digits. Mrs. Karen reminded her of her physical therapist, tough but kind, and always proud of her progress.

This time after surgery, she only had one cast change in the hospital. After that, Dr. Dehne decided to let her keep the same cast on for a month. Before long, she'd get a brace for her right leg, too. She imagined pulling on two socks, and two shoes, letting go of her walker, and walking. No more surgeries, no more casts, no more wheelchairs, no more going backward, and no more crawling, ever again.

> *Medea,*
> *You remember when you helped me walk?*
> *Remember how I leaned on your back and the sun made us*
> *sweat*
> *and the dirt was hot under our feet?*
> *Remember?*
> *It is hard sometimes*
> *to remember.*
> *It is hard sometimes,*
> *whispering to you in the dark*
> *and never hearing you whisper back.*

CHAPTER TWENTY-ONE

ONE SATURDAY MORNING, CLAY HOISTED A BAG OF MULCH OVER his shoulder and carried it to the backyard. There were bags and bags on the driveway, waiting to be opened and spread in the flower beds. Rebeka sat on the grass in the backyard and watched. It was a beautiful day, the sky blue and the temperature warm.

"Do you want to help?" Clay asked Rebeka.

"Yes!"

"We better protect your cast so it doesn't get dirty," said Meredith. She tied a plastic bag over it. "Let's take your brace off, so it stays clean, too."

"Dr. Bud says I don't take it off." She hadn't forgotten the rules. She didn't want her foot to droop.

"It will only be for a little while," said Meredith.

Rebeka looked down at her left foot. Her sock and her brace and her shoe formed a barrier between her still-tender foot and the rest of the world. "I get another bag for my brace."

Meredith sat back in the grass and hugged her knees. "What's going to happen when your foot gets too big for your brace and you can't wear it anymore? You need to make your foot tough so when that happens, it doesn't hurt without the brace."

Rebeka thought about how her knees and the backs of her hands used to be tough when she crawled everywhere. Then the tops of her feet got tough when she started walking on them. Now she needed to make the bottoms of her feet tough, and the side, and all the parts that hurt.

"Okay," Rebeka told Meredith. "I try."

She took off her shoe, pulled the straps off the Velcro, slid off the brace and her sock, and handed them to Meredith. She held her leg stiff, her foot suspended above the tickly grass. She wasn't quite ready to be tough yet. In a minute.

"Here, this is just your size," said Clay, handing her a small rake. "I'll dump the mulch and you rake it out of the pile so it's evenly spread. Ready?"

"Ready!"

Rebeka fiercely raking mulch.

She attacked the mulch pile from her spot sitting on the grass.

It felt good to be outside, good to use her body, good to have a job to do. It wasn't until all the mulch had been spread that she looked down and realized her foot was resting on the grass. It hardly hurt at all. Maybe all the therapy, and the brushing with the soft brush, and the scar rubbing, was finally working. That night, she brushed her foot just a little harder. When she rubbed the scar tissue, she pushed a little deeper.

"So what did you think about spreading the mulch?" asked Nate after dinner.

"It was good."

"Good? Spreading mulch is never good."

"It was good!" she insisted.

"No, french fries are good, video games are good, Disneyland is good, but mulch is never good!"

She had heard all about Disneyland because the Davises were taking her there. They explained that Disneyland was in a place called California, and they were going to ride in a plane and stay in a hotel and ride roller coasters and meet princesses and see snow and mountains and the ocean.

"Mulch is better than Disneyland," said Rebeka.

"You're just saying that because you haven't seen Disneyland yet."

"Mom, you should buy Rebeka a princess dress for the trip," said Alayna. "A Cinderella one. You remember that movie, Rebeka?"

"Doopity, doopity, doopity!" That's what the short old lady with the wand said before turning a pumpkin into a magic coach.

"No, it's bibbidi-bobbidi-boo!" said Alayna.

"Doopity, doopity, doopity!"

"Alayna, I wish you could go with us," said Meredith.

"Me, too. I want to see Rebeka's face when she sees the Disney castle!" Alayna picked up Rebeka and twirled her around. "You won't believe it!"

"Why you not go?" she asked.

"Remember? I told you. I'm going to Europe with my school at the same time. Don't worry, you'll have so much fun without me you'll forget I'm not there!"

"I never forget that," said Rebeka.

She was so excited she couldn't sleep the night before their flight to California. The next morning, she sat right next to the little oval window on the plane. On her flights to America from Rwanda, she had always sat in the middle so she never got to see outside. She pressed her forehead to the glass and watched the buildings get small. It was like there was a whole new world up high, where the clouds were huge and the blue sky went on as far as she could see.

When the plane landed, Nate pushed her through the busy airport in her wheelchair.

"Is this Disneyland?" she asked.

"No! This is just California."

They got their baggage and loaded up the rental car. "First stop, the beach!" said Clay. They drove for a while and then found a parking spot near the water. Clay wheeled her down a long wooden pier.

"This is the ocean," he said.

She gazed across the blue water, light blue and then darker farther out. It went on and on, with no land in sight, kind of like the sky up high in the airplane.

"It is big," she said. "So big." Looking at it made her feel small. They were all small compared with the giant ocean: Clay, Meredith, Nate, and Benji.

"Let's go to the beach!" yelled Benji. He kicked off his shoes and ran out into the sand. Meredith pulled a plastic bag out of her purse and Clay knelt down to tie it over Rebeka's cast so it wouldn't get wet. Then he took off the shoe, brace, and sock on her left foot.

"What are you doing?" she asked.

Clay didn't answer. He just picked her up and ran with her across the beach, right into the water. She shrieked as he bent down and dipped her toe into the freezing-cold water. "No!" She laughed and kicked her foot, splashing Clay.

"You're in the ocean!" said Clay. "What do you think?"

"It's big and wet and cold!"

He went to the sand and set her down. Her bare foot left a footprint. She stared at it, the way her five toes made five little dents and her heel made another big dent. Her footprint looked the same as any other footprint.

A wave washed up and erased her footprint and splashed Clay's shorts. He set her down farther up on the beach, next to Benji. They dug holes and built sandcastles. They watched kids flying kites, running up and down the beach. Rebeka imagined holding a kite, running on the bottoms of her two bare feet, leaving a trail of footprints in her path.

Rebeka and Clay in the ocean at Huntington Beach near Los Angeles, California.

141

It wouldn't be long before Dr. Dehne took off her cast and she got the brace for her right foot.

"Time to go," said Meredith. "It's getting dark."

They dusted off their clothes and headed to the hotel for dinner and then got ready for bed. They were all sleeping in one big room.

"Good night, Rebeka," said Clay. "Are you excited about Disneyland tomorrow?"

"Doopity, doopity, doopity!"

"Doopity, doopity!" Nate repeated, and then Benji, and everybody started laughing and doopity-dooping. Finally, the room got quiet and they all fell asleep.

Rebeka dressed as Minnie Mouse on the carousel at Disneyland in Anaheim, California.

The next morning, Rebeka put on the pink polka-dotted dress she'd worn for Halloween and her mouse ears, and they went to Disneyland. She wasn't a fan of the fast roller coasters; they made her feel like she was going to be sick, but she loved the merry-go-round. All of the Disney princesses signed her pink autograph book and her cast. Meredith took her shopping and they picked out the most beautiful dress she had ever seen. It was a real princess dress, with layers of soft lace and sparkles all over it. She put it on the next day and they went back to the park to ride more rides and meet more princesses. By dinnertime, everyone was covered in her sparkles.

The next day it was time for the mountains. They drove two hours, going up and up, and she got to see snow for the first time.

Rebeka sees snow for the first time in Big Bear Lake, California.

"Where are the flakes?" she asked, thinking of the snowflakes hanging from her ceiling back home. Mama had said each one was different, just like people.

"Everywhere!" said Benji. "They're all packed together, millions of them."

Rebeka leaned close to the snow, trying to see how each one was different from the other, but it was packed too tight. They all looked the same.

"Rebeka, this is how you make a snow angel!"

Nate showed her how to lie on her back and move her arms and legs up and down. Then they made a tiny snowman with rocks for eyes and sticks for a nose and mouth. On their last day, they visited an aquarium where sharks swam on the other side of a big piece of glass and colorful birds perched on Rebeka's arms and ate birdseed out of tiny paper cups.

"What was your favorite part of the trip?" Clay asked Rebeka on the plane back to Austin.

Rebeka thought about it all: her sparkly dress and the tiny snowman and the vast ocean. Next to the ocean, everyone was small. Everyone was the same.

"The ocean," said Rebeka. "I love the ocean."

> "Alayna, the ocean is very big. It does not stop. It was my favorite."
>
> "You liked it better than princesses?"
>
> "Yes. And better than snow."
>
> Alayna reached out and grabbed her hand. "I wish I could have gone with you."

"Me, too."

"I flew over the ocean to get to Europe for my trip. You're right. It is big."

Alayna fell asleep still holding her hand. Someday Rebeka would fly back over that big ocean. Back to Medea and Mama and Papa and home.

She closed her eyes.

For now, this was home. She squeezed Alayna's fingers gently.

Clay and Rebeka on Huntington Beach, California.

CHAPTER TWENTY-TWO

WHEN SHE GOT BACK FROM CALIFORNIA, IT WAS TIME TO have the cast on her right foot changed. Dr. Dehne had waited a whole month to give her incisions time to heal, hopeful it wouldn't hurt as much to take it off as the left one had. He bounded into the exam room all smiles and energy. "I'm thinking this is the last cast," he announced.

"What?" she asked.

"What?" Meredith asked.

"As long as it isn't too painful to have your foot exposed, I think your scars will heal faster with no cast."

He gently began to unwrap the bandages. Her foot was sore, yes, but not the searing, burning pain she felt with her left foot. When he was done, she reached down and carefully touched her foot, running her finger along the scars and pulling on her toes. She smiled. It had turned well, and it didn't hurt.

"Sometimes one foot is more sensitive than the other," said Dr. Dehne. "Her right foot looks great. No more casts!"

"No cast." Meredith put her arm around Rebeka's shoulders and gave her a big squeeze, and they rocked back and forth on the exam table. Gina took pictures of both of her turned-straight feet.

"How about we get some socks for your pretty new feet?" asked Meredith.

"Yes! Socks, please." She had been excited about socks ever since she'd seen Alayna's drawer full of them. She picked a pair of long ones that stretched to her knees, with different-colored polka dots. At home, Meredith helped her put them on. It hurt the tender skin on her left foot, especially the scars. Meredith opened the toe up wide so her foot could fit all the way in and then she let go of the sock all at once so it was one big hurt, instead of a bunch of tiny hurts.

A few days later, Meredith sat at the table where Rebeka was drawing pictures and took out the calendar they used to sing the days of the week and months of the year song. She took a deep breath. "I've been talking to Africa New Life, and we've picked a date for you to go home."

Home? It felt as if her heart stopped beating for a second. She looked at the crayon in her hand, the table where she sat, and her plate with beans and avocado in a tortilla. Nate's music was playing in the other room, the microwave dinged, the refrigerator hummed, and somewhere, someone flushed a toilet. She hadn't thought about home in a while.

Meredith took a red pen and circled June 24 on the calendar.

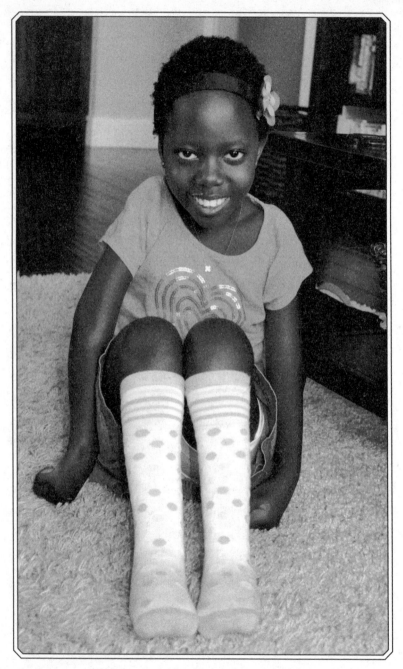

Rebeka in two socks after surgeries on both feet.

"That's the day you'll fly back to your family and your friends and your house and all the things you miss."

Rebeka stared at the red circle. She hadn't whispered to Medea at night in a long while. Home seemed so far away. The thought of going back didn't fill her with hope or joy. It filled her with fear.

"What if my feet turn again when I go back?"

"Dr. Dehne says the best way to prevent that is to keep walking. It's the most important thing you can do, and you can do that here or in Rwanda. I know it will be hard to say goodbye, but it's still a couple months away."

A couple months didn't feel like long enough. The Davises had begun to feel like family just as much as her family back in Rwanda. "There aren't the same kind of hospitals or doctors where I live," she said.

"Rebeka, don't worry. Dr. Dehne wouldn't send you home if you weren't ready. But it's important to remember to keep walking, and to keep rubbing your scars. Nobody is going to make you do these things back home, Rebeka. You must do them yourself."

Rebeka looked down at the calendar. There was nothing she could do. The date was circled in permanent red pen. She was going to have to leave everything that had become familiar, again.

She met with Katie twice a week, she kept brushing her feet so they were less sensitive, and she kept rubbing her scars so they wouldn't be lumpy and hard.

Her most important work was walking, though. She had come to realize she'd never walk like Medea or Kate, no matter how hard she practiced. She still had to use her hips to lift her legs, her knees were stiff, and her ankles weren't very flexible. But she could learn how

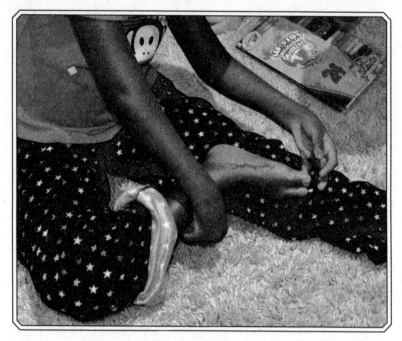

Rebeka showing her surgery scar on her right foot.

to walk faster and for longer, with practice, and that would have to be enough.

As long as she never crawled again, it was enough.

"It's time to start walking without your walker," Katie said at one appointment.

It was hard, letting go of the silver frame and learning how to balance, taking the full weight of her body on her two feet.

"Now it's time to practice walking without your braces," said Katie, once she could walk without her walker. "Even though you'll wear your braces until you grow out of them, it's good to practice without them so you'll be ready when they don't fit anymore."

More hard work. Rebeka practiced at home on the sidewalk in

front of the house, sometimes with her braces and walker, sometimes without.

Someone always went with her, to cheer and push the jog stroller in case she needed a break. Friends drove by and honked and waved and cheered out the car windows. Rebeka smiled and swung her arms to wave, but most of the time she wasn't smiling.

"It's boring to walk when I have nowhere to go," she said.

"Well, where do you want to go?" asked Clay.

Rebeka thought for a minute. "To Kate's!" She wanted to play with Kate, make some cookies, paint their nails, ride skateboards down the driveway . . . anything but practice taking step after painful step.

Rebeka walking down the sidewalk with her walker.

Clay was looking at something on his phone.

"Let me see," said Rebeka.

Clay tilted his phone so she could see that he was looking at a map. "It's almost exactly one mile from our house to Kate's. That isn't too far. You walked three miles to your school back home, and that was on the tops of your feet." Clay pointed to a spot on the map. "You've walked to the end of our street so far. I'd say that's about two-tenths of the way."

"Two-tenths?"

"Pretend we had ten giant cubes, kind of like the cubes you use with Mrs. Karen to do math. And pretend it took ten cubes to cover the distance from our house to Kate's. You've walked two cube distances so far. Just eight more to go!"

She looked down at her pink shoes, then back up at Clay. "I'll do it!" She finally had somewhere she wanted to go, instead of just walking to walk. "I'll walk to Kate's house."

Clay drew a map and broke the route into sections, each a tenth of a mile, or one cube.

Every time she went another section farther on her walk, she colored that part of the path with orange highlighter. At first, it took her over thirteen minutes to walk a cube. At that rate, it would take over two hours to walk to Kate's house, and she knew she wasn't strong enough to walk that long. She only had two months to reach her goal. Clay hung the map on the refrigerator, next to the picture of her family. Each step closer to Kate's house was a step closer to home. It made her happy, and it made her sad, all at the same time.

She kept walking, one foot in front of the other. One Tuesday evening, toward the end of May, she was starting a walk with Meredith when Alayna challenged her to a race. "I'll lunge and you walk," she said.

She took a giant step and bent her front leg until the knee of her back leg was almost touching the pavement. Then she took another giant step and did the same thing with the other leg. Before long, Alayna was breathing heavy and Rebeka passed her up. "Go Rebeka!" Meredith called. Rebeka gave Alayna a swat and kept going, working hard to get ahead. Alayna got left so far behind lunging that she had to yell to be heard. Rebeka threw back her head and laughed. She was filled with confidence and joy, beating Alayna on this cool spring night.

"I'm going to walk to Kate's house," she said as she hit the first cube length, the first of ten.

"That's right. Eventually you'll walk all the way to Kate's house," said Meredith. "Your record is seven-tenths of a mile so far, or seven cubes. That's over halfway!"

"I'm going to walk to Kate's house *now*," she said.

"Really?" said Meredith. "Go for it!"

It would be dark soon. If she was going to do this, she was going to have to keep up her pace. She didn't stop for her first rest until three cubes. By five cubes, she was sweating hard, and by cube six, it was completely dark outside.

"Are you sure you want to keep going?" asked Meredith.

"Yes!"

Every time she stopped to rest, Alayna started lunging again to get ahead, and Rebeka chased her down. Meredith pulled her phone out of her pocket.

"Clay? I think Rebeka is going all the way to Kate's tonight. You guys better come so you can cheer."

Clay and the boys came quickly. He parked his car on the side of the road and they all piled out. Clay called Kate, and she showed up on her bike to cheer, too. Rebeka was really tired. Her legs were shaky and she was breathing hard, but she couldn't stop now. She got closer and closer. Kate hurried into her house while everyone else lined up on either side of the sidewalk and cheered and clapped. Kate came back with a roll of toilet paper and they stretched it across the street, a homemade finish line.

When Rebeka was only a couple of houses away, she had a final burst of energy. Her arms were swinging as she practically ran through the finish line, victorious. The paper tore and drifted in the cool night wind like a long white streamer.

Nate lifted one of Rebeka's arms in the air, and Kate lifted the other.

"Victory!" they cheered. "You did it!"

She did it. It was harder than she thought, but she was stronger than she'd thought she was. "I did it!"

After they were done celebrating, they all loaded into Clay's car and drove home. Back in Rwanda, she wouldn't have the choice of a car. She would have to turn around and make the long walk home again. But she knew now that if she wanted it bad enough, she could get wherever she needed to go.

Medea,
I walked all the way to Kate's house.
But you don't know Kate, or her house.

You don't know my favorite spot on the shaggy rug in front
 of the fireplace,
you don't know that Molly likes her belly rubbed,
or that Clay is ticklish.
You know the old Rebeka,
but do you know me anymore, Medea?

CHAPTER TWENTY-THREE

THERE WERE MANY PARTIES IN JUNE BEFORE SHE FLEW HOME. On Rebeka's last visit to Dr. Dehne, she walked into an exam room to find a table decorated with a pink tablecloth and streamers. There was juice and cookies, and the nurses and ladies at the front desk, and of course Gina and Dr. Dehne, were all there to celebrate and say goodbye.

Rebeka was a different person from the scared little girl getting X-rays on her first visit. It wasn't just her turned-straight feet, or her hair that had grown full and thick, or her body that had grown healthy and round. She was different on the inside, too. She was braver and stronger, and that was good. She would need to be brave and strong to say goodbye.

She saw Katie one last time and they took videos so she could show her parents her exercises and how to rub her scars to make them soft.

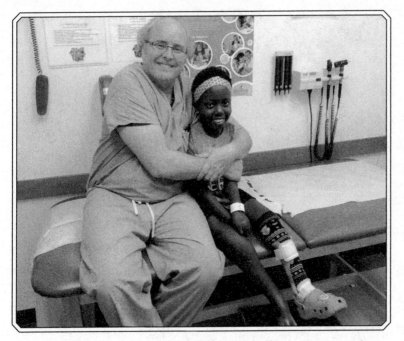

Rebeka and Dr. Dehne.

"I'm proud of you, Rebeka," said Katie. "You worked hard. Keep up the good work!" She turned to Meredith. "She's ready. She's learned to walk on her own two feet. Now all she has to do is keep walking."

"What did Katie mean," Rebeka asked on the way home, "when she said I learned to walk on my own two feet? I cannot walk with your feet, or Clay's feet." She laughed and shook her head. Meredith laughed, too.

"It's something we say in America. It means you can do things on your own, like learn English, make friends, and hang a hook on the wall for your tutu. When you go back to Rwanda, nobody can

Clay and Rebeka on the roof.

make you keep rubbing your scars, or stretching your toes, or walking when you're sore. It's up to you. But you've proved you can walk on your own two feet, so I know you can do it."

Once school let out, the Davises packed up so they could go back to the lake. Before they left, Clay showed her how to climb out the upstairs window and onto the roof of the house by the school. They sat there, side by side, looking out on the street below and the blue, blue sky above.

"The sky goes on and on, like the ocean," said Rebeka.

"It goes all the way to Rwanda, and beyond," said Clay.

At the lake, they had a party and all her friends came to say goodbye. Mrs. Karen brought her a few books to take home.

"Remember that first day I was your teacher, and I couldn't hear you, so I went to the other side of the room and made you shout?" she asked.

"Yes!"

"You came to America with almost no English words, and now you can read, Rebeka. I am so proud of you."

Everyone brought her gifts, small things that would fit in her overstuffed suitcase, which was already full of gifts for her family. She unwrapped socks, and a bracelet, and little toys called jibbitz to push through the holes in her shoes. Kate gave her a picture she

Clay and Rebeka on the boat dock.

Rebeka and her friend Ava, playing with minnows.

drew of the two of them standing next to each other. They had their arms around each other, friends forever, even across the ocean. They both cried when she left. After the party, Rebeka tucked her treasures into her suitcase.

There was one last boat ride, one last fish to catch, and one last run around the trampoline on her straightened-out feet.

She took one last long walk, almost a mile. Neighbors joined them from up and down the street. Someone blew bubbles, and someone else brought balloons, so that the walk felt more like another party than hard work. She held Alayna's hand when she got tired, and sweat dripped down her back, but she did it.

Benji, Rebeka, Alayna, and Nate on the tube.

Finally, it was the night before the day circled in red on the calendar. The Davises made stepping-stones by pressing Rebeka's flat foot into concrete to save its shape. It was cool and wet and reminded her of the sand on the beach in California. She helped press shells from the lake around the edges for decoration.

"Every time we see your footprint we'll remember you," said Meredith.

They gave her a photo album filled with pictures of her time in Austin. She blew out candles on a big cookie cake. That night, they had a sleepover, all tumbled together on the couch and a sleeping bag pallet in the middle of the living room. Once all the lights were out and it was

Alayna carving Rebeka's name on the stepping-stones.

dark in the room, she said, "Doopity, doopity," and everyone laughed and doopity-dooped until they fell asleep.

Very early the next morning, while it was still dark outside, the six of them got up for one last Uno game before heading to the airport. Rebeka won, of course. She almost always won. She tilted her chin and smiled her smile and did a little victory dance, while inside she felt as taut as a hungry goat's tether. She took shallow breaths and held her tears back by avoiding eye contact.

Clay, Rebeka, Meredith, Benji, Alayna, and Nate
at the Austin airport.

"Time to go," said Clay, looking at his phone. "The Simpaos are on their way to the airport."

She was flying home with the Simpao family. The dad was a doctor and they were moving to Rwanda so he could work at a hospital in the capital city. When they got to the airport, everyone tried hard not to cry.

Rebeka clutched her new backpack tight and rubbed her cheek on the soft collar of her fuzzy pink jacket. It was time to go home, to Medea, and Mama and Papa, and the red dirt roads, and the rolling green hills of Rwanda.

And so she was brave and strong and she said goodbye. There were tears, but the Davises promised to come and visit soon. She turned her gaze across the ocean. On June 24, she spread her wings, and strong as a butterfly, she got on an airplane and flew away home.

Alayna,
I wonder what you're doing right now?
I'm on the plane.
Soon I'll be back in Rwanda.
Will you really come and visit me?
If you do, you can meet Medea.
She is my favorite sister in Rwanda.
You are my favorite sister in America.

PART THREE

RWANDA

CHAPTER TWENTY-FOUR

W HEN THE PLANE TOUCHED DOWN IN KIGALI, RWANDA, REBEKA and the Simpaos waited until most of the people left before gathering their things and stepping out, into the night. Rebeka took a deep breath. It smelled like the diesel from motorcycles, the sweetness of mangoes, and the greenness of growing things. Mr. Simpao picked her up, carried her down the metal stairs that had been rolled up to the airplane, and set her gently in a wheelchair.

She wanted to stand up and walk through the airport, into Mama's arms, but first she had to wait in line for her passport to be checked. Then there was more waiting for her suitcase to be unloaded from the plane. The longer she waited, the more nervous she became. The chatter of Kinyarwanda all around her seemed like noise and nothing more. It had been so long since she'd spoken her language. She had turned it off, like water in a tap, so she could learn English. Now she didn't know how to turn the tap back on so she could understand what people were saying.

"Let's go!" Mrs. Simpao finally said, and pushed her wheelchair away from the crowd at baggage claim. Her backpack was a heavy weight in her lap, anchoring her to the wheelchair. As she was pushed around a corner, she saw them. Mama and Papa hurried forward and hugged her tight. Mama's shoulders were shaking. Rebeka breathed in her familiar smell. Papa's arms felt strong and familiar. Mama stepped back and looked at her carefully.

Rebeka slid from the wheelchair, letting her backpack fall, and stood up tall. She walked a short distance on the bottoms of her flat feet. Mama clapped her hands and then threw her arms in the air. *"Imana ishimwe!"* she cried. Then she asked a question, but her

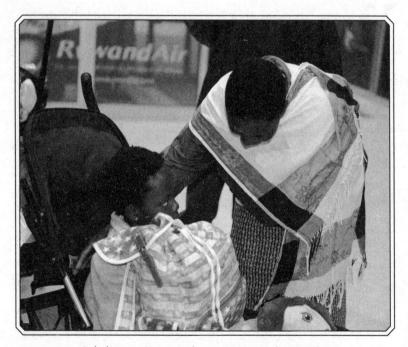

Rebeka sees Mama at the airport in Kigali, Rwanda.

Kinyarwanda words sounded strange and unfamiliar in Rebeka's ears. She couldn't understand what Mama was saying.

What was wrong with her? She opened her mouth, closed it again, opened and closed it like a fish out of water. Why couldn't she speak? Her eyes filled with tears.

That night she stayed with her parents in the Africa New Life mission house in Kigali. She showed her parents all the gifts in her two suitcases. She tried to tell them stories about her time in Austin, but every time she opened her mouth, only English came out. Once everything had settled down and the house was quiet, Mama carefully looked Rebeka over from head to toe.

"*Nkeneye kumenya neza ko uyu ar'umwana wange,*" Mama said. She studied her hands, middle finger to palm.

There was a woman at the guest house who spoke English and Kinyarwanda. "She says she needs to be certain you are her child!" said the woman, laughing.

"It's me, Mama!" said Rebeka. She turned to the woman. "What is wrong with me? Why can't I understand my parents?"

"I don't know," said the woman. She put a hand on Rebeka's head. "But don't worry. I'm sure it will come back to you. You just need to give it some time."

She had a hard time falling asleep that night, and she could hear Mama tossing and turning in the next bed while Papa snored. Mama was worried, too.

The next day, Rebeka chose her clothes carefully. She was going home, and she wanted to look her very best. She pulled on a bright pink shirt and her turquoise skirt made from feathery-light tulle. It fell in soft layers to her knees like the skirts the ballerinas in the

Mama and Rebeka after she returned to Rwanda.

Nutcracker wore. She pulled on a pair of black leggings to wear underneath. Then she slipped on a pink headband from Mrs. Karen and clipped on a soft yellow flower made of felt. She chose her long pink-and-gray-striped socks and fastened her braces with the purple butterflies over them. She liked the way the braces felt, strong and familiar. Last, she put on her bright pink shoes. The holes were filled with small toys from her friends in America. There was a horse, a letter "R," a glittery bow, hearts, princesses, a ladybug, fish, a pink Minnie Mouse, and of course a butterfly.

Finally, they piled into a van and drove away. Rebeka looked out the window at motorcycles swerving in and out of traffic, women carrying babies on their backs with baskets of bananas on their heads, and men pushing bicycles loaded down with yellow water jugs. Outside the city, they passed fields of maize, and avocado and mango trees. It all looked very, very different from Austin, Texas. It looked like home.

After about an hour, they turned off the paved road and onto one made of red dirt. It was a bumpy ride because the rainy season had just ended, leaving many dips and ditches in their path. She leaned into Mama, then Papa, as they were tossed back and forth in the van. The driver stopped next to the Kibenga school, where Rebeka had her classes before coming to America.

"What are we doing here?" asked Rebeka in English. Mama just stared back at her, unable to understand or answer.

"Just a quick visit," the driver said.

A large crowd of students circled their car, all wearing their red-and-white-checkered shirts, the girls in red skirts and the boys in red shorts. Her stomach churned. She was led to the front porch of the building by the headmaster, while the students chattered and pointed. As she stood in front of the crowd, and the headmaster put his hand on her shoulder, she felt a mango-sized lump in her throat.

Did they expect her to say something?

Even if she could manage to say a few words, they would be in English.

She looked all around with wide eyes, her heart racing as fast as the motorboat at the lake house in Texas. Luckily, the headmaster was the one who spoke. Her parents stood nearby, Mama smiling with pride and Papa watching while his hands opened and closed, opened and closed. She could tell he was nervous, too.

"Rebeka went to America for treatment," the headmaster said in

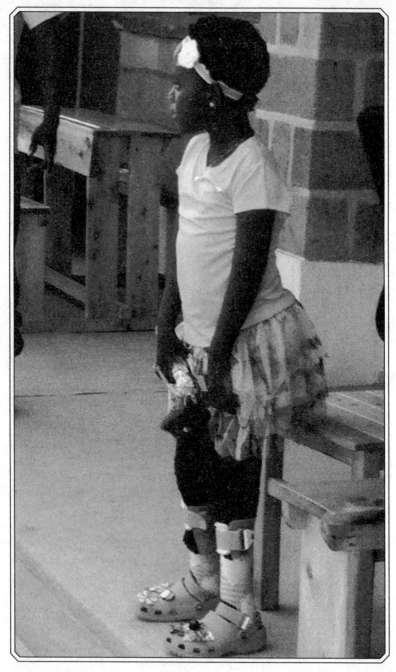
Rebeka at the school in Bugesera, looking at all the students.

English. He pointed to her feet and continued, "We thank God that she is now fine." Then he repeated it in Kinyarwanda, and everyone clapped and cheered.

Rebeka's chest swelled with pride as she realized they were cheering for her.

As the students went back to their classes, a few of them stopped Rebeka and tried to talk to her. She didn't understand what they were saying but she smiled and nodded her head and said, "See you later."

She got back in the car with Mama and Papa and they drove to their house. They passed the market where Mama bought oil and soap, passed fields of maize and stacks of mud bricks drying in the sun for someone's house, and finally she saw the lake. They were almost there!

But wait . . . there was a large crowd gathered outside her home. As they stepped out of the car, people rushed up to them.

"*Ikaze murugo!*"

"*Twishimiye kubona Rebeka abasha kugenda.*"

"*Numukobwa ukomeye!*"

"What are they saying?" Rebeka asked their driver.

"They say welcome home, and that they are happy to see you walking, and that you look strong."

Rebeka looked at the crowd and smiled. Then she saw Medea standing inside the door to the courtyard. She seemed shy, and a little scared. Rebeka hurried over and slipped her hand into Medea's, who looked at her with curious eyes. She asked a question, but Rebeka couldn't understand. She squeezed her hand instead and tried not to cry.

That night, when the sun went down, it was time for bed. There was no electricity to turn on a light. Rebeka walked under the stars to the bathroom. Then she snuggled into bed next to Medea.

Rebeka and Medea.

Medea, what do you think of my new feet?

Sinumva imby'umbwira.

Medea, I can't understand you.

Sinumva icyuvuga.

"My name is Rebeka," she said, slowly and carefully.

"My name is Medea," said Medea in English.

"I am ten years old," said Rebeka.

"I am eight years old," said Medea.

"I love you."

"Ndagukunda."

CHAPTER TWENTY-FIVE

F OR THE NEXT FEW WEEKS, REBEKA SPENT A LOT OF TIME SITTING quietly and listening to her family chatter all around her.

Mama, Papa, and Rebeka standing outside their home in Bugesera.

Slowly, slowly, the mango-sized lump in her throat grew smaller. She said one word in Kinyarwanda, and then another. Just as she learned to walk, step by step, and just as she had learned English, Rebeka learned to speak her language again, word by word.

It took about three weeks, but finally she got most of her Kinyarwanda back. Then her words came tumbling out, stories about life in Texas, trampolines and boat rides and grocery stores with shelves full of food. She could carry on a conversation in English or Kinyarwanda. She helped Medea learn more English words, teaching the sister who had once taught her letters and numbers with chalk on the concrete floor.

As she lived day to day, falling back into some of her old routines, there was one big difference. Instead of being left behind, she was always surrounded by a crowd of kids, asking her questions about America in Kinyarwanda. She could understand them now and give them answers.

"What is it like in America?"

"How bad does surgery hurt?"

"Do they have beans and rice?"

"America is big and beautiful and strange." They laughed. "Surgery hurts very bad. And yes, they have beans and rice and avocados and mangoes, but they also have french fries!" She told them about dogs that lived inside the house and football games and the ocean that went on and on, as far as the eye could see.

Things weren't perfect being back in Rwanda. Some people still made fun of the way she walked. Some were jealous of her time in America. But her world was much bigger than rude comments or pointing fingers. She was a storyteller, an English speaker, a book reader, a princess, a go-kart driver, and so much more. If she started to feel lonely or left out, she reminded herself of all her friends in America who loved her, and all the hours she worked hard to learn to walk. She knew she was brave and strong and a good friend, so mean words didn't hurt so much anymore.

But there was something that would always be difficult. Her school was three miles from her home. If she couldn't get a ride on a bicycle, she had to walk, and she arrived late and exhausted. Even though she was walking on the bottoms of her feet, she was still slow. Her knees and hips weren't very flexible, so she walked stiff-legged and tired easily.

One day, a woman from Africa New Life came to talk to Mama and Papa, just like the day when she found out she was going to America. She sat by the woman's side on the couch, listening carefully.

"We would like to enroll Rebeka at the New Life Christian Academy in Kayonza," she said.

Rebeka bit her lip. She had heard of the New Life Academy. Everyone had. It was very competitive, one of the top schools in the country. It was also several hours from her home by car.

"If she goes there," the woman continued, "Rebeka can live on campus in one of the dormitories and walk just a few steps to get to her classes instead of three miles. She will live in a home with seventeen other girls and a house mother, she will get three good meals a day, and she will receive an excellent education. All the teachers there speak very good English."

Across the small coffee table, her mother clasped her hands under her chin, and her father nodded his head thoughtfully.

"What do you think, Rebeka?" asked Papa.

"I think it will be hard to leave you again." She dug her finger into her palm. "But chance comes once, Papa. Maybe I should take this chance."

Papa reached out a hand and grabbed hers. "We will miss you, but this is the right choice. You will have wonderful teachers, and your future will be bright." He turned to the woman. "We are thankful for this opportunity."

And so it was decided. Rebeka was excited and sad at the same time. Medea cried when she heard. "You are leaving me again," she said. "You are always leaving."

All her life, Rebeka thought she was the one being left behind, but now she looked at the world through Medea's eyes. She realized it had been just as hard for Medea when she left for America, and now for boarding school.

"I am sorry," she told her sister. "It is hard for me, too. Believing that chances only come once helped me to be brave enough to go to America, and now boarding school." She handed Medea a piece of chalk. "You have the chance to teach Dukudane and Uwiteka their letters, just like you taught me. It may be their only chance to learn, and you are a very good teacher. I don't know what I would have done without you."

When she first moved to the boarding school in Kayonza, it was hard.

She was very quiet as she watched the other students and tried to figure out this new world. The girls in her dormitory were kind. They helped her with her tray in the lunchroom since she couldn't carry it, they walked with her to class, and they listened to her stories. She told them about

Rebeka taking a nap at her boarding school, New Life Christian Academy in Kayonza, Rwanda.

growing up with twisted feet, her time in America, casts and surgeries and new friends and the ocean, and then coming home again. Before long she was laughing and chatting. She was the same Rebeka, but different.

Time passed. After a few months, she was performing at the top of her class, placing third out of fifty-seven her first semester. She missed her family, but she knew this was where she was supposed to be. And then one day, a van came to the boarding school and drove her to the airport. This time she was the one waiting when the Davises came around the corner, visiting from America.

They drove to her home in Bugesera to meet her family, and she showed them her snowflakes, hanging from the ceiling. Papa had

Left to right: Uwiteka, Dukudane, Medea, Mama, and Rebeka in their home, Bugesera, Rwanda.

also hung pictures of her friends from Austin and some of the small toys she got in America. With the help of a translator and Rebeka, the Davises and her family began to talk.

When it was time for the Davises to go, Meredith and Mama cried a little, and they hugged for a long time.

"*Murakoze*," said Mama.

"We love Rebeka," said Meredith. "We are so proud of her. You raised a brave, strong girl." Rebeka translated, and Mama cried some more.

The Davises had gotten special permission to take her out of school for a few days so she could stay with them at the guest house

Rebeka and Alayna in Rwanda.

Rebeka in her school uniform, standing near dorms at New Life Christian Academy in Kayonza, Rwanda.

and ride on the bus to meet some of their other sponsored children. She showed them her boarding school and they explored the rolling green hills of Rwanda together.

Their visit made her feel a little mixed up inside. It made her long for America and all her friends, even though she loved her family and friends in her own country, too. When they brought Rebeka back to her house and they had to say goodbye, she cried. When Medea saw her tears, she cried, too.

"We'll be back. I promise," said Meredith.

They took one last picture, both families together, and then they were gone.

Rebeka dried her tears, rubbing her cheeks with her shoulders. She would see the Davises again. She turned her eyes to the lake on

181

Left to right, back row: Alayna, Nate, Papa, Clay, Esperanze, Mama; front row: Rebeka, Benji, Meredith, Medea.

the horizon, the lake she couldn't see when she lived her life on the ground, crawling. She would not live her days in sadness. She had a choice to make each day, and that chance came only once. She would choose joy.

At boarding school, she slept in a room with five other girls, their metal bunk beds stacked three girls high. Soft night sounds filled the room, the creak of a bed, the flush of a toilet, and the deep breathing of her new friend Sharon, sleeping above her. A warm breeze drifted through the open window and brushed Rebeka's cheeks, soft as a butterfly's wings. She reached down and traced the shape of her turned-straight feet under her blanket. Everybody was asleep, and she would be soon, but first, she needed to tell Medea good night.

> *Medea,*
> *I miss you.*
> *I know that life can be hard at home,*
> *no toilet,*
> *water to fetch,*
> *and a long, long walk to school.*
> *But hardest of all, for you and for me,*
> *is that we are many miles apart.*
> *Life is hard, like the pit of a mango,*
> *but it is sweet, too,*
> *sweet as mango juice*
> *dripping down our chins as we sat in the garden,*
> *when I learned how to walk for the very first time.*
> *You are sweeter than mangoes, Medea,*
> *stronger than the pit.*
> Ndagukunda.

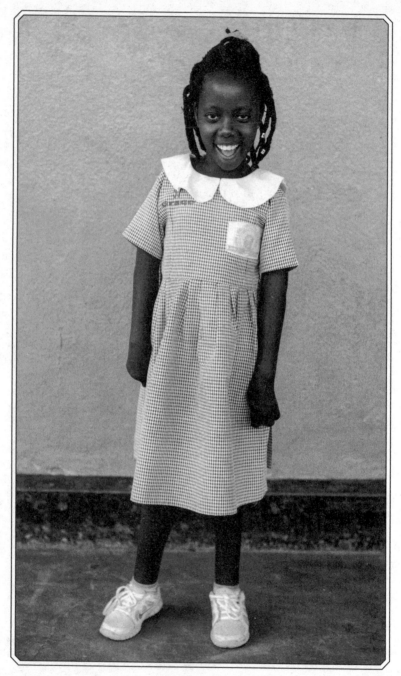

Rebeka, age 11, in her New Life Christian
Academy uniform.

GLOSSARY

Translations were provided by Augustine Ndemezo, who accompanied Meredith during interviews. The **bold** syllables are the stressed syllables, those which receive emphasis. To hear Rebeka read each of these phrases, go to herowntwofeet.com.

Kinyarwanda Words

*Amakuru [ah-muh-**koo**-roo]*: How are you?

*Imana ishimwe [ee-**mah**-nee **shim**-wuh]*: Praise God!

*Murabeho [**more**-uh-**bay**-hoe]*: goodbye

*Muraho [more-**ah**-ho]*: hello

*Murakoze [more-a-**koh**-zay]*: thank you

*Muzungu [moo-**zoon**-goo]*: a foreigner, generally a white person

*Mwaramutse [**mwahr**-uh-**moot**-say]*: good morning

*Ndagukunda [n-**dah**-gah-**koon**-duh]*: I love you.

*Ni meza [nee-**may**-zuh]*: I am fine.

*Sawa [**sah**-wah]*: okay

*Seka [**say**-kuh]*: smile

*Seka cyane [**say**-kuh **chah**-nay]*: smile big

*Uwitonze [oo-wi-**tone**-zay]*: peace

*Wihangane [wee-**hahn**-gah-nay]*: I'm sorry, try to bear this.

Kinyarwanda Sentences

*Amahirwe aza rimwe [ah-**mah-hee**-gway **ah**-zah **reem**-way]*:
Chance comes once.

*Uzandindishavu Nzakubebishema [oo-**zan**-deen-di-**shah**-voo n-**zah**-koo-bay-bi-**shim**-ah]*:
Protect me from grief. I will be your pride.

*Nkeneye kumenya neza ko uyu ar'umwana wange [nuh-**nay**-yah **koo**-min-yah **nay**-zah koh oo-**you** arum-**wah**-nah wong]*:
I need to be certain this is my child.

*Ikaze murugo! [i-**kah**-zah more-oo-goo]*:
Welcome home!

*Twishimiye kubona Rebeka abasha kugenda! [twish-**eem**-way koo-**bone**-ah Rebeka ah-**bosh**-ah koo-**jen**-duh]*:
We are so happy to see Rebeka able to walk!

*Numukobwa ukomeye! [noo-moo-**koh**-bwah oo-**kome**-yay]*:
She is so strong!

*Rebeka, sinumva imby'umbwira [Rebeka, sin-**oom**-vah ib-yo ohm-**gee**-ray]*:
Rebeka, I can't understand you.

*Sinumva icyuvuga [sin-**oom**-vah itchy-**voo**-guh]*:
I don't know what you are saying.

A NOTE FROM REBEKA

I hope people who read my story will be encouraged. I was born the way God created me. I endured hard things. If I can do it, you can do it.

When I was little, people used to tell me bad things. I heard them tell my parents that they should not keep me. Kids used to say they wouldn't play with me because I looked different than them. I would tell them, "I cannot force you to be my friend." Then I would go home and tell my parents, and they would say, "God has a plan for you." So I prayed hard, and God helped me.

Not everyone was mean to me. My family loved me, and I had some friends. One of those friends was Niyonkuru. She lived in a house nearby, and she walked with Medea and me to school. She used to tell the others, "This girl is nice. She didn't create herself. If you don't want to walk with us, go. We will walk alone."

Now I am in school and I have many friends, including Sharon and Grace and Agnes. When I first arrived at the boarding school in Kayonza, they saw me sitting by myself. I was afraid because I didn't know anybody. My heart told me I would never find a friend, but they came up to me and asked me my name. They told me about my new school, that it was good, and they said they loved new people. They taught me some of the Kinyarwanda words I didn't remember, and they helped me wash my clothes and carry my tray in the dining hall. My mom and dad visited after a few weeks and I was happy again.

At school when they teach about children who are born different, they tell the students to talk to me. I tell them that I am okay. I tell them about how my feet used to look and about my time in America, and my surgeries, and that I was brave and other kids can be brave, too.

I am learning lots of new things at school. I loved learning about the heart, and how it pumps blood through the body, including the lungs, where it gets oxygen. I want to be a doctor when I grow up. I would hear other kids talking about what they wanted to be when I was little, and I decided I want to help people. That will be good. I went through many troubles and I want to help those who are like me and tell them not to worry, it will be okay.

I want to thank Africa New Life for welcoming me to the New Life Christian Academy in Kayonza. When I was young, they helped me to get a sponsor that helped me with my problems. When Meredith told me her idea about writing a book, I was excited because my life would not be forgotten. It will remind me again and again about my story, and I say thank you.

A NOTE FROM MEREDITH

Our family started sponsoring kids through Africa New Life Ministries (ANLM) years before Rebeka came to live with us in 2012. We had even traveled to Rwanda a couple of times to meet our sponsored kids. While we were there, we had no idea that in a village south of the capital city of Kigali, there was a little girl drawing letters with chalk on the concrete floor of her home, wishing she could go to school.

About eight months before Rebeka came to America, my husband, Clay, hosted a seminar for small business owners in Rwanda. One day, before the seminar started, he hopped in a van with a woman who was going to meet her sponsored child, Medeatrece. While everyone was busy hugging and unpacking the bag of gifts, Clay noticed Medeatrece's sister Rebeka. She had twisted feet and a beautiful smile. He offered Rebeka a sucker, never guessing that she would come to America and live with us for almost a year.

Clay called me that night and told me about the little girl he met. He was eager to sponsor her so she could go to school. But it turned out that another family had sponsored her back in Austin, a family we happened to know, whose kids went to our kids' school, and whose father was a doctor in Austin. They chose Rebeka because she had the same birthday as one of their daughters, Ani. It was incredible, all these things coming together. Rebeka could have been sponsored by a family in Portland, New York, or London. The family could have never found out she had disabilities, and even if they did, they may not have had any way they could help.

But that isn't what happened. When Clay got back home, he showed Dr. Rice pictures and videos of Rebeka. Dr. Rice was shocked. He had no idea Rebeka had a disability. He began having conversations with a hospital where he worked, and a few months later we got a call from ANLM, asking if we would be Rebeka's host family. A private foundation would pay for all of her doctor and hospital costs. She just needed a place to stay.

Nobody could tell us if the doctors would be able to treat her, or how long the treatments would last. They had to examine her first. We would have to wait and see. We were just as afraid as Rebeka as we all stepped into the unknown, but "chance comes once," and we didn't want to miss out on what could be an amazing story.

We were impressed by Rebeka's bravery and resilience. She left her family and all that was familiar, she flew on a plane across the ocean, and she came to live with strangers who spoke another language. She was terrified of dogs, couldn't swim, and had a deathly fear of needles, but she came anyway. She confronted her fear by taking life day by day and embracing each new experience. By the time she left, she had worn thirty-one different casts and gone to the hospital fifty-eight times. I want other kids to be inspired by her story and realize that they can be brave and strong, too, no matter what life might throw at them.

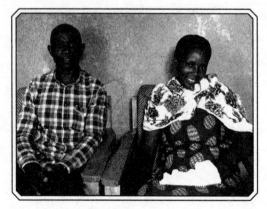

Rebeka's papa and mama.

When I started writing this book, I knew it wasn't just my story to tell. I would need Rebeka's help and the help of many others. Rebeka was eager to collaborate. She wanted to share her story, but she didn't have all the

English words she needed. Neither did I. After living with her for nearly a year, I knew Rebeka was ticklish and fiercely competitive and did not like vegetables. But there was much I didn't know about Rebeka's early childhood, and her life at the boarding school after she returned to Rwanda.

Meredith's translator, Augustine Ndemezo, showing Rebeka's file.

I booked a ticket to Rwanda, my sixth visit to that beautiful country of rolling green hills and red dirt roads. I interviewed her parents, her teachers, headmasters, friends, a mama in her boarding school, and anyone else I could find who knew Rebeka when she was young, before she came to America, and after she came home again.

And of course, I interviewed Rebeka. She showed me the bed she and Medea shared, and introduced me to her friends at boarding school.

When I got back home, I studied the hundreds of pictures from Rebeka's time in America and reread all the blog entries and the daily journal I kept while she was with us.

Meredith with Rebbeka Kabatesi, the child sponsorship coordinator with ANLM who told Rebeka and her parents she could go to the US, and to boarding school.

191

Rebeka with her kindergarten teacher, Beza Rehema.

Rebeka's parents have only two pictures of her before the age of nine. Cameras were a luxury for people who lived in rural Rwanda, and there was no easy way to have a picture printed. Those two pictures are pressed between the pages of her mother's Bible, a treasure for her and for me.

I listened to my taped interviews again and again. Once Rebeka's story was written, and rewritten, and rewritten again, I had it recorded in Kinyarwanda and sent it to Rebeka and her parents with small portable CD players so they could hear and understand every word. A few weeks later, I traveled to Rwanda again and listened to their comments and edited until it became the story you hold in your hands: *Her Own Two Feet.*

Rebeka sitting on the bed she and Medea shared in her home.

I chose to leave many things out of Rebeka's story, and the story of Rwanda. Eight years before Rebeka's birth, a terrible genocide raged through her country. In one hundred days, almost a million people were slaughtered. Miraculously, Rebeka's parents survived. They did not allow fear to drive their decisions when Rebeka was born. They did not listen when their neighbors encouraged them to kill their disabled daughter. They chose love.

Rebeka with friends Grace (left) and Sharon (right).

Today, Rwanda has recovered remarkably from the genocide. Many dealt with their grief and loss with forgiveness and reconciliation. Africa New Life Ministries began in response to the many children orphaned because of the genocide. Orphaned and poor children needed stability. They needed a place where they could grow and thrive. They needed school. Africa New Life found sponsors to support their education.

What you hold right now is as close to Rebeka's truth as I could get. With Rebeka's help, I imagined what went through her mind as she sat by the side of the road when she was little, how she felt when her parents left her alone in a clinic for eight months when she was only four years old, and how her heart must

Rebeka and Meredith holding the first page from a draft of this book.

have pounded in her chest when our dog jumped on her bed her first night in Austin.

It is in the listening and imagining, creeping into someone else's head and heart, that we truly come to understand each other's stories. It is how we go from strangers to friends. It is an honor to call Rebeka a friend.

ACKNOWLEDGMENTS

Rebeka and I owe a huge debt of gratitude to many people. We'd like to thank Augustine Ndemezo, who accompanied me and translated during the interviews, Rebbeka Kabatesi for her advice and help in translating and bearing witness to Rebeka's transformation when returning from America, and Cyusa Lionel, who translated and recorded the manuscript into Kinyarwanda so Rebeka and her parents could hear every word.

Also thanks to Rebeka's kindergarten teacher, Beza Rehema, for her kindness, her interview, and insight; to Rebeka's first house mother in Kayonza, Jovia Kibibi; and to Beatrice Karamgwa for translating my phone interview with Jovia. Thanks to Anna Kyomugisha, who traveled with Rebeka to Austin along with her baby, Danny, and to her husband, Rev. Fred Isaac Katagwa, and to Specioza Dusabe Mukazaire, who helped me communicate with Rebeka long-distance. Additional thanks to Fred Karwanyi, who helped Rebeka get her visa and paperwork and showed me her files; to Ntirenganya Jovan, who drove me safely to interviews; to Nizeyimana Jean Piere, the child development officer for ANLM in Bugesera who has a fondness for Shakespeare and a generous spirit; and to Dr. Charles Mugisha, who dreams big dreams and lives his faith with boldness and authenticity. *Murakoze cyane.*

We also thank Natalie Green, who lives in two worlds and makes so many amazing things happen, and Betty Davis, who checked in on Rebeka once she returned to Rwanda. Also to Mark and Kayan Simpao, who took Rebeka home again, got her good shoes, and answered our questions about her feet and overall health.

We also thank the kind people at Dell Children's Medical Center of Central Texas, especially Dr. Robert Dehne; his assistant, Gina Wilhm; Arie "Bud" Bronkhorst, who made Rebeka's braces; and physical therapist Katie Navarro. In addition, thanks to then-president Sister Teresa George, and for the generosity of all the doctors, nurses, assistants, and technicians who donated their services so Rebeka could walk on the bottoms of her feet. We are so grateful.

Rebeka and I would like to thank all of our Austin friends and the time they spent with Rebeka, including frequent play dates with Natalie Green, the Brocks, the Clarks, the Rices (Rebeka's sponsors), the Daehlers, Elizabeth Giddens, and the Berlangas, with special thanks to Mrs. Karen, Rebeka's teacher. Also to all the kind families on Mañana Street: Breedlove, Griggs, Hausmann, Hodge, Houtz, Miller, Trenasty, Wilkens and Yacktman. And in Travis Country, so many including: Adams, Allen, Anderson, Cobb, Duncan, George, Gonzales, Grace, Minter, Norwood, Ray, Rodgers, Spencer and Wise. It takes a village. You supported us and prayed for us, and we thank you.

We would like to thank Rebeka's family in Rwanda: her parents, Patricia and Anastase; her brother, Emmanuel; and sisters Magwaneza, Uwase, Esperanze, Medeatrece, Uwiteka, and Dukudane. We also thank family in Texas, including Maurice and Peggy Davis, Louise Davis, Bernie and JoBeth Grall, Dick Davis, Joe Limon, Uncle Craig and Aunt Rhonda, McKenzie and Brant Davis, Marvin and Sharen Eggleston, Uncle David and Aunt Leslie, Wyatt, Emma, and Claire Erfurt.

In addition, I have some writing folk I need to thank. From the very beginning, there was Kathi Appelt, Anne Bustard, Betty Davis, and Cynthia Leitich Smith. I thank the Society of Children's Book Writers and Illustrators, who allowed us to start an Austin chapter. It attracted talented writers and illustrators like bees to honey. Along came so many good friends, encouragers, and fellow creatives, too many to name them all, but I must mention Lindsey Lane, Lindsey Scheibe, Bethany Hegedus, Paige Britt, Jerri Romine, and Gayleen Rabakukk, who is a fellow Bat Poet graduate of Vermont College of Fine Arts, class of 2011, and faithful weekly writing companion. I am thankful for all the Bat Poets, and the outstanding faculty and students who make VCFA a magical place. To my advisors Ellen Howard, Kathi Appelt, Martine Leavitt, and Susan Fletcher, your fingerprints are all over my writing. And to Bunmi Ishola, who read an early version and provided valuable feedback.

A special thank-you to my agent, Alyssa Eisner Henkin, who believed in this project from the very beginning. She is an amazing champion. And to Amanda Shih, who said yes with such enthusiasm I knew this book had found its perfect home. All the fine folks at Scholastic have my gratitude for their hard work and careful attention to this story.

Thanks to my kids, Alayna, Nate, and Benji, who think of Rebeka as another sister. They love her story, and they cheered loud and long when they learned it would be shared. And to my husband, Clay Davis. He says yes to adventure and uncertainty and embraces change. Without his encouragement, I would not be who I am today. He inspires me. *Ndagukunda.*

And last, Rebeka and I want to thank the One from whom all blessings flow, and all good stories, too. *Imana ishimwe!*

ABOUT AFRICA NEW LIFE MINISTRIES

Africa New Life Ministries (ANLM) enables donors to sponsor Rwandan children like Medea and Rebeka so they can go to school. A monthly donation pays for tuition, uniforms, scholastic materials, and basic medical assistance. Fifty percent of the net proceeds of this book will be donated to ANLM. If you would like to find out more, visit africanewlife.org.

ABOUT THE AUTHORS

MEREDITH DAVIS worked at an independent children's bookstore and started the Austin chapter of the Society of Children's Book Writers and Illustrators before earning her MFA in Writing for Children and Young Adults from Vermont College of Fine Arts. She lives and writes in Austin, Texas. This is her debut book.

REBEKA UWITONZE goes to school in Kayonza, Rwanda, and spends her holidays at her home in Bugesera. She was born with arthrogryposis, a disease that caused her joints to contract, resulting in stiffness, clubfeet, and muscle atrophy in her arms. This is her debut book, in which she is able to share her inspiring story with the world.

To find out more about Rebeka, go to
herowntwofeet.com.